THE ENCHIRIDION

From Lesson To Action!

EPICTETUS

Adapted For Today's Reader By Sam Nusselt

∎∎∎

List of Contributors: Epictetus, Elizabeth Carter

Epictetus was a Greek philosopher who lived from 55-135 AD. He was born into slavery in Hierapolis, Phrygia (present-day Turkey) and later gained his freedom. Epictetus' teachings were centered around Stoicism, emphasizing the importance of self-discipline, acceptance of fate, and the pursuit of virtue. Although he did not write any of his teachings, his pupil Arrian, a Roman senator, compiled the "Discourses" and the "Enchiridion" based on Epictetus' lectures. Epictetus' philosophy had a major influence on later Stoic philosophers and continues to be studied and respected to this day.

THE ENCHIRIDION – From Lesson To Action!

Adaptation, Cover, Copyright © 2023 by SAM NUSSELT

Cover Art/Image: Created Under Commercial License from Midjourney Inc. At 18/07/2023. Terms Of Service Version Effective Date: July 21, 2023.

All rights reserved. No part of this book may be used or reproduced in any manner whatsoever without prior written permission.

Edition/Version: 1/7 [Revised 4 June 2024]

1. Ethics.   2. Stoics.   3. Life.

■ ΑΩ ■

Disclaimer: Please note that the information contained in this document is for educational and entertainment purposes only. Every effort has been made to present accurate, up-to-date, reliable and complete information. No warranty of any kind is expressed or implied. Readers acknowledge that the author is not engaged in rendering legal, financial, medical or professional advice. The contents of this book have been researched from & various sources. Please consult a licensed practitioner before attempting any of the techniques described in this book. By reading this document, the reader accepts that under no circumstances can the author be held responsible for any loss, direct or indirect, suffered as a result of the use of the information contained in this document, including, but not limited to, errors, omissions or inaccuracies.

Expand your literary horizons and gift the joy of reading:
Discover a world of captivating books that inspire, educate,
and entertain!

https://www.legendaryeditions.art/

CONTENTS

CHAPTER 1 — WHAT IS IN OUR CONTROL 1

    Achieving True Freedom and Happiness by Acknowledging and Accepting What is Within Our Control 1
    Finding Happiness by Shifting Focus to Controllable Desires 4
    Appreciating the Essence of Things and Relationships 5
    Using Mental Preparation to Stay Aligned with Your Core Values 5
    The Power of Personal Judgments and Growth 6
    Finding True Accomplishment: Embracing Humility and Taking Control of Your Actions 7
    Prioritizing the Bigger Picture: Navigating Life and the Ship 9

CHAPTER 2 — HOW TO ACT APPROPRIATELY 11

    Embracing Acceptance: Finding Tranquility in Life's Unpredictability 11
    Overcoming Illness: The Power of persevering Morals 13
    Developing Inner Strength: Resisting External Influences 14
    The Concept of Loss and Ownership 16
    Embracing Peace of Mind and Abandoning Material Concerns 17
    Balancing Authenticity and Impression Management 18

CHAPTER 3 — MASTERING IMPRESSIONS 21

    The Power of Controlling Your Desires and Avoiding Disappointment 21
    Approaching Life with Grace and Patience: The Path to Deserving Greatness ... 22
    The Interpretation of Distress: Understanding Emotional Reactions 24
    The Power of the Playwright: Embrace Your Assigned Role 25
    The Power of Perception in Interpreting Signs and Omens 25
    Finding True Happiness and Freedom: The Power of Controlling What You Can 27
    Taking Control of Your Emotions: The Power of Perception 27

CONTENTS

EMBRACING DEATH AND CULTIVATING A POSITIVE MINDSET 29
THE CHALLENGES OF PURSUING PHILOSOPHY 30

CHAPTER 4 — MENTAL PREPARATION 31

EMBRACING INNER WISDOM: THE PATH TO LIVING A PURPOSEFUL LIFE 31
LIVING A LIFE OF HONOR AND SIGNIFICANCE 32
THE IMPORTANCE OF MANAGING EXPECTATIONS AND PURSUING INDIVIDUAL PATHS 34
TREAT YOURSELF WITH COMPASSION AND UNDERSTANDING 36
THE SIGNIFICANCE OF EVIL IN THE WORLD 37
THE VULNERABILITY OF YOUR MIND: ARE YOU GIVING IT AWAY TOO EASILY? 39
CHOOSING YOUR PATH: THE IMPORTANCE OF CONSIDERATION AND COMMITMENT 40
NAVIGATING SOCIAL RESPONSIBILITIES: THE POWER OF RELATIONSHIPS AND SELF-REFLECTION 42

CHAPTER 5 — SOCIAL ROLES AND DUTIES 45

THE IMPORTANCE OF BELIEFS AND MINDSET IN DEVOTION TO THE GODS 45
THE ROLE OF DIVINATION AND REASON IN DECISION-MAKING 47
SETTING A STRONG AND NOBLE CHARACTER: GUIDELINES FOR ENGAGING WITH OTHERS 48
NAVIGATING PLEASURE: FINDING BALANCE AND RESISTING TEMPTATION 52
EMBRACE YOUR BELIEFS AND OVERCOME JUDGEMENT 54
FINDING BALANCE BETWEEN SELF-CARE AND SOCIAL CONTEXT AT THE DINNER TABLE 55
THE CONSEQUENCES OF TAKING ON UNATTAINABLE ROLES 56
PROTECTING YOUR INNER GUIDANCE: A KEY TO WELL-BEING AND SAFE NAVIGATION 57
PROPORTIONAL POSSESSIONS: MAINTAINING BALANCE AND AVOIDING EXCESS 58

CHAPTER 6 — MENTAL FORTITUDE AND APPROPRIATE ACTIONS 61

EMPOWERING YOUNG WOMEN: MOVING BEYOND APPEARANCE 61
BALANCING PHYSICAL AND MENTAL WELL-BEING 63
NAVIGATING NEGATIVE INTERACTIONS: UNDERSTANDING OTHERS' PERSPECTIVES 64
APPROACHING CONFLICT WITH COMPASSION: HANDLING DIFFICULT SITUATIONS WITH FAMILY 66
MAKING SENSE OF STATEMENTS: MOVING BEYOND SURFACE COMPARISONS 67
UNDERSTANDING MOTIVES: THE IMPORTANCE OF AVOIDING JUDGEMENT 68
EMBODYING PHILOSOPHICAL PRINCIPLES THROUGH ACTIONS 69
EMBRACING SIMPLICITY: THE POWER OF DISCRETION IN SELF-CARE 70
SEEKING PROGRESS: TAKING RESPONSIBILITY AND LETTING GO OF EXTERNAL INFLUENCES 71
FINDING TRUE UNDERSTANDING: BEYOND INTERPRETATION AND INTO ACTION 73

EMBRACING UNBREAKABLE PRINCIPLES AND IGNORING OPINIONS OF OTHERS 74
CLAIM YOUR WORTH AND ACHIEVE PROGRESS: EMBRACE SELF-IMPROVEMENT AND LIVE WITH PURPOSE 75
LIVING BY PHILOSOPHICAL PRINCIPLES ,,,,,,,,, ... 76
THE POWER OF SPIRITUAL CONNECTION AND RESILIENCE 78

INDEX **81**

PREFACE

Welcome, to the profound and transformative journey that lies within these pages.

In this volume, we embark upon an exploration of the timeless wisdom of Epictetus, one of the most influential Stoic philosophers of all time. Inspired by the needs and challenges of the modern reader, this guide beautifully aligns ancient Stoic philosophy with the complexities and demands of our contemporary world.

Enter a world where the profound words of Epictetus are skillfully presented and adapted to resonate with your soul. Dive deep into the beguiling realm of Stoic principles as they are brought to life through insightful analysis and a fresh perspective on their application in our everyday lives.

Drawing from the concise and invaluable manual written by Epictetus himself, known as the Enchiridion, we lay the groundwork for this transformative journey. With utmost care and reverence, the author explores the essential tenets of Stoicism, guiding us towards a more meaningful and virtuous existence.

Explore the power of acceptance, of understanding what lies within our control and what does not. Delve into the pursuit of self-mastery, and the art of embracing gratitude. As the author illuminates these profound concepts, we are met with relatable examples and conveyed in a conversational and accessible style that ensures the seamless assimilation of Stoic principles into our daily lives.

However, this guide is not simply a repository of knowledge. It is a call to action, an invitation to embark on a transformative odyssey of self-reflection and self-improvement. With thought-provoking exercises and prompts, the author empowers us to internalize Stoic

PREFACE

teachings, uncover our true potential, and embrace a life of fulfillment and tranquility.

As you journey through the reading, you will not only encounter the wisdom of the ancients, but you will discover a compass to navigate the challenges of our modern era with clarity, purpose, and grace.

Welcome to the ultimate Stoicism guide. May it serve as your steadfast companion on this remarkable voyage of self-discovery and personal transformation.

CHAPTER 1

— What Is in Our Control

In this opening chapter, Epictetus lays the groundwork for Stoic philosophy by emphasizing the significance of understanding what we can and cannot control. He urges us to focus our energy on our own thoughts, decisions, and preferences, rather than being consumed by external factors such as money, social status, and physical well-being, which are outside our control. By adopting this mindset, we can discover genuine freedom and inner peace in our lives.

> Achieving True Freedom and Happiness by Acknowledging and Accepting What is Within Our Control

1. Sometimes, we have control over certain things in our lives, while other things are simply out of our control. The things we can control include our choices, desires, and actions - essentially, anything that is within our power. On the other hand, the things we cannot control are things like our physical bodies, our belongings, our reputation, and our position in society - basically, anything that we have no influence over.

It is important to recognize that the things we can control are naturally unrestricted and unaffected by external factors, while the things we cannot control are vulnerable, subservient, and easily influenced by external circumstances. So, it's crucial to understand that if we start considering something that is inherently restrictive as something free, or if we start claiming something that is not ours as

Chapter 1 — What Is in Our Control

our own, we will only limit ourselves, feel frustrated, be in a constant state of unrest, and place blame on both others and ourselves.

However, if we acknowledge only what is truly our own as such, and what is not our own as what it really is, then no one will ever be able to force us to do something against our will, no one will hold us back, we won't blame or find fault with anyone, we won't do anything against our desires, we won't have any personal enemies, and no one will be able to harm us because nothing can truly harm us.

With such lofty aspirations in mind, it is important to remember that achieving them will require significant effort on our part. We may have to let go of some things completely and postpone others for the moment. But if we desire both these things and material success, such as wealth and status, it is possible that we will not attain even the latter because we are also focusing on the former. And ultimately, we will fail to achieve the true freedom and happiness that only come through the pursuit of those higher goals.

Therefore, from the very beginning, make it a habit to address any negative external influences by acknowledging that they are external and not truly what they seem. Then, evaluate and analyze them using the criteria you have developed, with the most important being whether the situation is within your control or not. And if it pertains to something beyond your control, be prepared to respond with the realization that it does not affect you personally.

From lesson...

Recognize what you can and cannot control, and focus your efforts on the things within your power to achieve true freedom and happiness.

To action!

(1) Recognize the things that are within your control, such as your choices, desires, and actions.
(2) Understand that external factors cannot restrict or have an impact on the things that you have control over.
(3) Differentiate between what truly is yours and what does not, while resisting the temptation to assert ownership over things that are beyond your control.

(4) Avoid limiting yourself by considering restrictive things as free or claiming something that is not yours as your own.
(5) Accept that things beyond your control are inherently vulnerable and easily influenced by external circumstances.
(6) Avoid placing blame on others or yourself for matters that are beyond your control.
(7) Acknowledge what truly is yours and what does not, and do not let anyone coerce you into doing something against your will.
(8) Do not allow external influences to hinder your progress towards your personal goals or hold you back.
(9) Refrain from blaming others for circumstances that are outside their control.
(10) Align your actions with your desires, and refrain from engaging in anything that contradicts your genuine desires.
(11) Cultivate a mindset that avoids creating personal enemies, as doing so only hinders your path to true freedom and happiness.
(12) Realize that nothing can truly harm you if you understand and accept the limitations of things beyond your control.
(13) Understand that achieving your aspirations requires significant effort and may involve temporarily or completely letting go of certain things.
(14) It is important to acknowledge that placing equal emphasis on personal growth and material success might impede the achievement of either goal.
(15) Strive for genuine freedom and happiness by pursuing loftier aspirations instead of solely fixating on riches and social standing.
(16) Develop the habit of addressing negative external influences by acknowledging their external nature and recognizing their lack of true impact on you.
(17) Evaluate and analyze external influences, considering whether or not they are within your control.
(18) When faced with circumstances that are out of your control, it is important to respond with the understanding that they do not have a personal impact on you.

Chapter 1 — What Is in Our Control

> Finding Happiness by Shifting Focus to Controllable Desires

2. Remember, the key to achieving your desires is to focus on what you want while avoiding what you do not. If you fail to attain what you desire, it is unfortunate, and if you end up experiencing what you wanted to avoid, it is a misfortune. However, this only applies to things that are within your control. Trying to avoid things like disease, death, or poverty, which are beyond your control, will only lead to misfortune. Instead, redirect your aversion towards things that are unnatural and controllable.

But for now, let go of your desires completely. If you desire something that is beyond your control, you are destined to be unhappy. Furthermore, the things that are within your control and would be beneficial to desire are not easily attainable. So, instead, focus on making choices and refusals, but do so lightly and without unnecessary pressure on yourself.

From lesson...

Focus on your desires and avoid what you do not want. However, this principle should only be applied to things that are within your control. Redirect any aversion you may feel towards things that you can actually influence, rather than wasting energy on uncontrollable and unnatural aspects. Additionally, it is crucial to let go of desires that are beyond your control to avoid unhappiness and unnecessary pressure.

To action!

(1) Focus on your desires and avoid what you do not want.
(2) Understand that failing to achieve desired outcomes is unfortunate, while experiencing what you wanted to avoid is considered misfortune.
(3) Recognize that certain things, such as disease, death, and poverty, are beyond your control, and attempting to evade them might result in misfortune.
(4) Redirect your aversion towards objects that are unnatural and controllable.
(5) Let go of desires that are beyond your control to prevent unhappiness.

Chapter 1 — What Is in Our Control

(6) Instead, concentrate on making decisions and exercising your power to say no when it comes to matters that are within your control.

(7) Do it with ease and without putting unnecessary pressure on yourself.

Appreciating the Essence of Things and Relationships

3. As you engage with things that bring you joy, serve a purpose, or hold sentimental value, take a moment to reflect on their essence. Begin with even the smallest things and ask yourself, "What is their true nature?" For instance, if you have a favorite mug, acknowledge your fondness for it, understanding that if it were to break, it would not upset you too severely. Similarly, when you show affection to your child or spouse, remind yourself that you are embracing a fellow human being, so that in the event of a tragedy, you will not be completely devastated.

From lesson...

Take a moment to reflect on the true essence and fleeting nature of the things that hold dear to you. This would help you evade the overwhelming devastation that inevitably follows when you lose them.

To action!

(1) Take a moment to reflect on the essence of things that bring you joy, serve a purpose, or hold sentimental value.

(2) Start by examining even the tiniest of things and inquire, "What is their true essence?"

(3) Acknowledge your fondness for your favorite items and remind yourself that losing them will not devastate you.

(4) Show affection to your loved ones and remind yourself that they too are fellow human beings.

(5) To effectively handle potential tragedies, it is crucial to mentally prepare yourself by nurturing a realistic perspective.

Using Mental Preparation to Stay Aligned with Your Core Values

4. Before embarking on any task, take a moment to consider exactly what you are getting yourself into. If you are planning to go

Chapter 1 — What Is in Our Control

for a swim, imagine the potential chaos that could unfold at a busy public pool - people splashing you, accidentally bumping into you, or even engaging in negative conversation or attempting to take your spot. By envisioning this scenario, you will mentally prepare yourself to address the task while remaining true to your principles. Apply this approach to any undertaking you embark upon. This way, if anything disrupts your plans at the pool, you will be able to brush it off and remind yourself that your objective was not only to swim but also to uphold your core values. Becoming excessively agitated about the situation will not aid you in achieving that.

From lesson...

When undertaking any task, it is important to consider the possible obstacles and disruptions that may come your way. By mentally preparing yourself and staying focused on your core values, you can avoid unnecessary frustration and maintain your trajectory towards your goals.

To action!

(1) Before diving in, take a moment to consider the task at hand.
(2) Imagine potential challenges or disruptions that may occur during the task.
(3) Psychologically, prepare yourself to take on the task while remaining faithful to your principles.
(4) Apply this approach to any endeavor or task that you undertake.
(5) Remind yourself that your goal is not only to complete the task at hand, but also to remain aligned with your core values.
(6) Do not let any disruptions or challenges that may arise bother you, instead choose to shrug them off and avoid getting worked up over them.
(7) Stay focused on achieving your goals and remaining true to your values instead of becoming entangled in external factors.

The Power of Personal Judgments and Growth

5. It is not the actual things themselves that bother people, but rather their opinions about those things. Take death, for example - it is not inherently scary; otherwise, Socrates would have thought so too. What is terrifying is the belief that death is something to be

feared. So, when we face obstacles, disruptions, or sadness, let us not point fingers at others. Instead, let us take responsibility for our own judgments. Blaming others for our problems is something an ignorant person does. Acknowledging our own faults is a sign that we are learning and growing. But the real mark of someone with true knowledge is neither blaming others nor blaming themselves.

From lesson...

Take responsibility for your own judgments, acknowledge your own faults, and refrain from blaming others or yourself for genuine knowledge and personal growth.

To action!

(1) Take a moment to reflect on your own opinions and beliefs about certain topics that may trouble you, such as death.
(2) Challenge the belief that death is inherently scary and examine whether our own judgment is causing fear.
(3) Rather than placing blame on others, we should instead accept responsibility for our own judgments when encountering obstacles, disruptions, or feelings of sadness.
(4) Recognize that blaming others for our problems is ignorant behavior and aim to avoid engaging in it.
(5) Acknowledging our own faults and mistakes is a true sign of personal growth and an opportunity for learning.
(6) Strive to neither allocate blame to others nor to ourselves, as this serves as an indication of genuine wisdom and comprehension.

Finding True Accomplishment: Embracing Humility and Taking Control of Your Actions

6. Don't become too proud of achievements that are not truly your own. It is one thing for a horse to feel proud and claim, "I am beautiful," but when you begin boasting about owning a beautiful horse, you are simply taking pride in something good that belongs to the horse, not yourself. So, what do you actually have control over? How you handle the circumstances that come your way. When you are capable of handling life's ups and downs in a manner that aligns with your values, then you can feel proud. That is when you can

Chapter 1 — What Is in Our Control

genuinely take credit for something positive in your life and experience a sense of accomplishment.

From lesson...

Do not claim credit for achievements that are not your own; instead, focus on how you face life's challenges to truly experience a sense of accomplishment.

To action!

(1) Reflect on your own achievements and give credit where it is due. Only claim credit for accomplishments that you have personally contributed to or played a significant role in.

(2) Practice humility by acknowledging and appreciating the achievements of others. Avoid stealing their credit or trying to take recognition for their hard work.

(3) Instead of seeking external validation through claiming credit, shift your focus on personal growth and overcoming challenges. Embrace the process of self-improvement and finding satisfaction in your own personal accomplishments.

(4) Develop a mindset of resilience and determination when facing life's challenges. Instead of avoiding or shying away from difficult situations, actively seek them out as opportunities for growth.

(5) Celebrate the successes and accomplishments of others genuinely. Offer support, encouragement, and recognition to those who deserve it, fostering a positive and collaborative environment.

(6) Cultivate awareness of your own limitations and areas for improvement. Focus on self-development and continuous learning to enhance your own abilities and increase your chances of genuine achievement.

(7) Explore new avenues for personal growth and develop new skills and talents. Embrace challenges outside your comfort zone, allowing for personal growth and a genuine sense of accomplishment.

(8) Foster a mindset of integrity and honesty. When faced with the temptation to claim credit unjustly or exaggerate your accomplishments, choose the path of authenticity and truthfulness.

(9) Seek feedback and constructive criticism from others. Embrace opportunities for learning and growth by actively seeking input from mentors, peers, or experts in your field.

(10) Celebrate and acknowledge the accomplishments of your team or collaborators. Recognize that collective achievements often involve the contributions and efforts of multiple individuals, and ensure credit is shared appropriately.

Prioritizing the Bigger Picture: Navigating Life and the Ship

7. Imagine you are on a voyage and your ship has anchored. You decide to go ashore to get some fresh water. Along the way, you come across a small sea creature or a tiny plant bulb that catches your eye. But here is the thing: you cannot get too caught up in exploring because you need to stay focused on the ship. After all, the captain might call for you at any moment, and if they do, you must drop everything and rush back to the ship. Trust me, you do not want to end up being tied up and thrown on board like a helpless sheep.

This scenario also applies to life itself. Let us say instead of a sea creature or a plant bulb, you have a little family, a loving partner, and a child. That is wonderful, no doubt. But remember, if the captain calls, you need to be ready to let go of it all and hurry back to the ship. Do not even think about looking back; just run as fast as you can.

Now, if you are an older person, it is even more important to stay close to the ship. You do not want to wander too far away because if the captain calls, you definitely do not want to miss it. So, keep yourself within reach, just in case.

In conclusion, whether you are on a ship or navigating life, it is crucial to prioritize what truly matters. Enjoy the little things along the way, but always keep an eye on the bigger picture and be ready to respond when it calls for you.

From lesson...

Prioritize what truly matters, appreciate the trivial things, but always be prepared to act when the bigger picture demands your attention.

To action!

(1) Stay focused on your main objective, whether it is obtaining fresh water on the voyage or fulfilling your responsibilities in life. Always keep your main goal in mind.

(2) Avoid getting too caught up in distractions: While it is tempting to explore and discover new things, remember to prioritize your obligations, and not get too engrossed in mere distractions.

(3) Be responsive to calls for action: in both the voyage and in life, be prepared to respond promptly when duty calls. Do not procrastinate or delay in attending to important tasks or responsibilities.

(4) Don't dwell on the past. When the captain calls, whether it is a significant hazard or a crucial situation, be ready to let go of whatever you cherish and move forward without any hesitation.

(5) Stay connected and within reach: If you are older, make sure to stay accessible and close to your responsibilities. Keep yourself engaged and available so that you do not miss notable events or calls for action.

(6) Prioritize what truly matters: While it is important to enjoy the little things along the way, always keep the bigger picture in mind. Prioritize what truly matters to achieve your goals and fulfill your responsibilities.

CHAPTER 2

— How to Act Appropriately

Epictetus shares valuable Stoic wisdom on how to live a virtuous life in various situations. He emphasizes the importance of fulfilling our responsibilities, displaying kindness to others, and effectively handling challenges and tough times. Epictetus highlights the role that our desires and aversions play in shaping our actions, and urges us to maintain a level-headed mindset in both success and disappointment. By adhering to these teachings, we can navigate through life with a sense of purpose and decency, making a positive impact on ourselves and those around us. So, let us delve into the exploration of how we can apply these timeless principles to our modern lives.

Embracing Acceptance: Finding Tranquility in Life's Unpredictability

8. Don't always expect everything to go exactly the way you want it to. Instead, accept that things will happen as they do and find peace in that. When you embrace this mindset, your life will become more tranquil and calmer.

From lesson...

Embrace uncertainty and find contentment in the natural unpredictability of life.

Chapter 2 — How to Act Appropriately

To action!

(1) Practice acceptance: Recognize that not everything will go according to your plans and expectations. Instead of resisting or becoming frustrated, choose to accept the reality of the situation.

(2) Let go of control: Understand that you cannot control every aspect of life. Learn to surrender to the flow of events and trust that things will work out in their own way.

(3) Cultivate a peaceful mindset by focusing on finding inner peace and tranquility. Engage in activities such as meditation, mindfulness, or yoga to help calm the mind and reduce stress.

(4) Embrace uncertainty: Embrace the unknown and unpredictability of life. Rather than fearing uncertainty, consider it as an opportunity for personal growth and new experiences.

(5) Shift your perspective: Adopt a more positive and flexible outlook on life. Instead of dwelling on what went wrong or what you did not get, focus on the present moment, and find gratitude for what you do have.

(6) Practice letting go of attachments: Avoid becoming too attached to specific outcomes or desires. Instead, detach yourself from the need for things to go a certain way and find contentment in the present moment.

(7) Adapt and adjust: When things do not go as planned, it is crucial to be adaptable and open to change. Instead of getting stuck in resistance, actively seek out alternative solutions or ways to navigate through challenges.

(8) Seek support: Surround yourself with a supportive community or seek guidance from a mentor or therapist who can help you navigate tough times and embrace a more accepting mindset.

(9) Practice self-care: Take care of yourself physically, mentally, and emotionally. Engage in activities that bring you joy and recharge your energy, helping you to better cope with life's inevitable difficulties.

(10) Focus on personal growth: Use setbacks or unexpected events as opportunities for personal growth and self-improvement. Embrace the lessons learned from any situation and utilize them to become a stronger, wiser individual.

Chapter 2 — How to Act Appropriately

> **Overcoming Illness: The Power of persevering Morals**

9. Illness can slow down our bodies, but it does not have to affect our morals, unless we allow it to. Being unable to walk properly might hinder our mobility, but it does not have to hinder our moral compass. Remember this whenever adversity strikes because you will realize that while it may impede one aspect of your life, it does not have to impede your authentic self.

> *From lesson...*

Do not let illness or adversity hinder your moral compass or true essence.

> *To action!*

(1) Take a moment to ponder your personal values and moral compass. Allocate some time to contemplate what deeply holds significance to you and the fundamental principles you strive to live by. Engaging in this process of self-reflection will assist you in fortifying your moral compass.

(2) Separate illness from character: Understand that being ill does not define your character or who you are as a person. Your true self is not determined by your physical condition.

(3) Practice resilience and determination: Despite any setbacks or physical limitations caused by illness, make a commitment to uphold your moral values and act in accordance with them. Cultivate resilience to overcome any obstacles that may arise.

(4) Seek support and inspiration: Surround yourself with positive influences and seek support from friends, family, or a support group. They can encourage and inspire you to stay true to your values, even during challenging times.

(5) Maintain a positive mindset: Focus on the aspects of your life that remain unaffected by illness and embrace an optimistic outlook. Remember that your moral compass can guide you through any difficulties you may face.

(6) Adapt your actions, not your morals. While physical abilities may change due to illness, it is crucial to ensure that your actions and choices still align with your moral compass. Seek alternative ways to express your values and contribute positively to the world.

Chapter 2 — How to Act Appropriately

(7) Embracing self-care is crucial: by taking care of both your physical and mental well-being, you will enhance your ability to uphold your morals in the face of any challenges brought on by illness. Make it a priority to engage in self-care activities that rejuvenate and fortify your mind, body, and spirit.
(8) Educate others about your condition: By sharing your experiences with others, you can enhance their understanding and empathy towards individuals facing similar challenges. This, in turn, can create a more inclusive and supportive environment for all.
(9) Inspire and advocate for others: Use your personal journey to inspire and empower others who may be struggling with illness or facing setbacks. Advocate for equality and accessibility for individuals with disabilities or health conditions.
(10) Find purpose and meaning: Discover how your experiences with illness can shape your purpose in life. Use this newfound clarity to live in alignment with your values and make a positive impact on your community and society.

Developing Inner Strength: Resisting External Influences

10. When faced with any situation, always take a moment to reflect on your own abilities to handle it. For instance, if you encounter an attractive person, it is crucial to practice self-control. When faced with difficult tasks, it is important to focus on developing your endurance. And when someone insults you, it is essential to cultivate the ability to remain patient and not let their words affect you. By training yourself in this way, you will not be easily swayed by external influences.

From lesson...

Take a moment to reflect on your abilities, practice self-control, and develop endurance. Cultivate patience and, above all, do not allow others' words to affect you. By adopting these principles, you will remain strong and unaffected by external influences.

To action!

(1) Take a moment to reflect on your own abilities when you are faced with any situation.

Chapter 2 — How to Act Appropriately

(2) When you find yourself in the presence of an attractive person, it is important to exercise self-control.

(3) Focus on developing your endurance when faced with challenging tasks.

(4) In life, we often encounter tasks that are difficult and demanding. These tasks can test our patience and resilience. Instead of feeling overwhelmed, it is important to focus on building our endurance.

(5) Endurance is the ability to persist and maintain our effort over a prolonged period of time, even when faced with obstacles. By focusing on endurance, we can improve our ability to handle difficult tasks and achieve success.

(6) There are several ways to develop endurance. One effective method is to break down the task into smaller, more manageable steps. This allows us to tackle the task gradually, building up our stamina along the way. By setting achievable goals and working consistently towards them, we can gradually increase our endurance and overcome challenges.

(7) Another way to develop endurance is through practice and repetition. Just as athletes train their bodies to perform at their best, we can train our minds to overcome difficulties. By repeatedly facing and conquering challenging tasks, we become more accustomed to adversity and develop the mental stamina necessary to succeed.

(8) Additionally, maintaining a positive attitude and believing in ourselves can greatly impact our endurance. When faced with difficult tasks, it is easy to feel discouraged or doubt our abilities. However, by maintaining a positive mindset and reminding ourselves of our past successes, we can cultivate the mental strength needed to push through obstacles.

(9) In conclusion, developing endurance is crucial for navigating and conquering difficult tasks. By breaking down tasks into smaller steps, practicing resilience, and maintaining a positive attitude, we can build our endurance and overcome any challenge that comes our way.

(10) Cultivate the ability to remain patient when someone insults you.

(11) Don't let the words of others affect you.

(12) Train yourself to become less easily swayed by external influences.

The Concept of Loss and Ownership

11. Never say that you have lost something, but only that you have given it back. Has your child passed away? They have been given back. Has your spouse passed away? They have been given back. "My farm was taken away from me." All right, even that has been given back. "But it was a scoundrel who took it!" But why does it matter to you who the Giver used to take it back? As long as He gives it to you, take care of it like it is not yours, just like travelers treat their temporary lodging.

From lesson...

Accept the losses in life as gifts from The Giver and appreciate them by treating what you are given with care, as if it is only temporary.

To action!

(1) Reframe loss as a form of giving back: Shift your mindset from perceiving it as a loss to acknowledging that it has been given back to you. By doing so, you can cultivate a more positive outlook towards challenging circumstances.
(2) Acceptance of loss: Understand that loss is a part of life and accept the reality of losing loved ones or possessions. By acknowledging this, you can start the healing process and move forward.
(3) Let go of attachments: Recognize that everything in life is temporary, and holding on to attachments can cause unnecessary suffering. Instead, practice detachment by treating everything as temporary and not fully belonging to you.
(4) Instead of dwelling on what you have lost, shift your focus to appreciating and taking care of what you currently have. This shift in perspective can cultivate gratitude and contentment in your life.
(5) Don't dwell on who caused the loss. Instead of fixating on the person responsible for your loss, let go of resentment and focus on the fact that the loss has been returned to you. Directing your energy towards anger or blame will only hinder your ability to move forward.

(6) Embrace impermanence: Understand and accept the transient nature of life, relationships, and possessions. This mindset can lead to greater resilience and adaptability when facing losses.

(7) Treat what you have with care: Just as travelers treat their temporary lodging, take care of what you have as if it were not truly yours. Cultivate a sense of responsibility and appreciation for the present moment.

(8) Practice non-attachment: Avoid becoming excessively attached to possessions, relationships, or circumstances. Instead, cultivate an attitude of non-attachment that enables you to navigate through life's changes with grace and equanimity.

(9) Reflect on the source of gifts: Consider the notion that everything, be it what is taken away or what is given back, originates from a higher power or the universe. Take a moment to contemplate this source and have faith in its grand plan for your life.

(10) Find peace in surrender: Accept that loss is a part of life's journey, and discover peace in surrendering to the natural flow of life. This acceptance can cultivate inner peace and a profound sense of freedom.

Embracing Peace of Mind and Abandoning Material Concerns

12. If you want to make progress, forget about reasoning like this: "If I neglect my responsibilities, I won't have any money to live on." "If I don't punish my employees, they will become unruly." It is better to face hunger while feeling free from sorrow and fear than to have an abundance of material things but be constantly troubled. Moreover, it is better for you to be unhappy than for your employees to misbehave. So, start with the small things. If some of your oil spills or your wine gets stolen, remind yourself, "This is the price I pay for a peaceful mind and tranquility." Remember, nothing comes without a cost. When you call your employees, bear in mind that they might not listen to you, and even if they do, they might not do what you want. However, their actions should not determine your peace of mind.

Chapter 2 — How to Act Appropriately

> *From lesson...*
> Focus on finding inner peace and tranquility, instead of being consumed by material possessions or the actions of others.

> *To action!*

(1) Shift your mindset and place greater importance on cultivating inner peace and tranquility, rather than focusing solely on material possessions and external circumstances.
(2) Start by addressing small challenges and inconveniences with a positive mindset, reminding yourself that they are the necessary costs for maintaining a peaceful mind.
(3) Adjust your expectations when it comes to your employees' behavior and actions. Understand that you cannot control them, and their actions should not disturb your peace of mind.
(4) Focus on your own actions and reactions instead of attempting to control the actions of others.
(5) Embrace the idea that it is better for your employees to misbehave or be unruly than for you to be unhappy. Prioritize your own happiness and well-being.
(6) When confronted with negligence of responsibilities, remind yourself that it is preferable to experience hunger while feeling free from sorrow and fear, rather than possessing an abundance of material things but constantly being troubled.
(7) Accept that progress may not always be easy or without sacrifices, but the pursuit of inner peace and tranquility is utterly worth it.
(8) Remember that nothing comes without a cost, and sometimes that cost may include minor setbacks or losses.
(9) Practice detachment from external circumstances and focus on cultivating a peaceful mind, regardless of the situation.
(10) Understand that you cannot control everything, and trying to do so will only create unnecessary stress and unhappiness. Instead, prioritize finding peace within yourself.

Balancing Authenticity and Impression Management

13. If you want to make progress in life, be okay with seeming silly or clueless on the surface. Do not worry about impressing others with your knowledge. And even if people view you as important,

Chapter 2 — How to Act Appropriately

remain humble. It is important to understand that staying true to your values while caring about others' opinions is not an easy task. It is like juggling, and if you focus solely on one aspect, you will inevitably neglect the other.

From lesson...

It is crucial to prioritize staying true to your values rather than worrying about the opinions of others.

To action!

(1) Embrace being silly or clueless; instead of fearing to ask questions or admit when you do not know something, actively seek opportunities to learn and grow. Embrace the concept that it is perfectly fine to not have all the answers and be receptive to new perspectives and knowledge.

(2) Shift your focus from impressing others to personal growth: Instead of constantly trying to prove your knowledge or skills to others, redirect your attention towards personal development and improvement. Set goals for yourself and wholeheartedly work towards achieving them, regardless of others' opinions.

(3) Practice humility: Even if others perceive you as important or knowledgeable, strive to remain humble and grounded. Acknowledge that there is always more to learn and that no one is perfect. Avoid being overly confident and instead, be open to receiving feedback and working on self-improvement.

(4) Stay true to your values: Identify your core values and beliefs and prioritize them in decision-making and actions. Do not compromise your principles or values to please others or gain their approval.

(5) Find balance: Recognize that there is a delicate balance between staying true to yourself and considering what others think. Strive to find the equilibrium that enables you to preserve your authenticity while also being mindful of the potential impact your actions and decisions may have on others.

(6) Prioritize self-awareness: Regularly reflect on your thoughts, actions, and motives. This self-awareness will help you navigate the balancing act between staying true to your values and caring about others' opinions. Understand why you make certain choices and assess if they align with your values.

Chapter 2 — How to Act Appropriately

(7) Be open to different perspectives: Engage in conversations and discussions with others who may have different viewpoints or expertise. This will help broaden your understanding and challenge your own beliefs while staying open-minded. Avoid becoming rigid in your thinking.

(8) Focus on personal progress and growth. Instead of seeking validation or approval from others, prioritize your own progress and development. Set goals, track your achievements, and celebrate your accomplishments, irrespective of external recognition.

(9) Accept and learn from failure: Understand that failure is a natural part of the learning and growth process. Embrace it as an opportunity to acquire valuable experiences and insights. Be resilient and take the time to learn from your mistakes, instead of fixating on them or seeking validation from others.

(10) Surround yourself with supportive individuals: Seek out a network of friends, mentors, or colleagues who support your growth and values. Surrounding yourself with like-minded individuals who encourage and inspire you can make it easier to stay true to yourself while also considering others' opinions.

CHAPTER 3

— Mastering Impressions

According to Epictetus, it is not the actual events that bother us, but rather how we perceive and evaluate those events. He suggests that we should scrutinize our initial impressions of what is taking place, abstain from categorizing things as good or bad, and endeavor to regulate our emotional responses. By doing this, we can enhance our ability to manage our thoughts and emotions.

The Power of Controlling Your Desires and Avoiding Disappointment

14. If you wish for your children, wife, and friends to live forever, well, that may seem a bit silly. Essentially, you are desiring something that is beyond your control and attempting to possess what does not rightfully belong to you. Similarly, if you harbor the hope that your slave-boy will embody perfection and be devoid of any faults, you are being foolish. To put it simply, you are essentially attempting to redefine vice as something other than vice.

However, here is the important part: if you want to avoid disappointment and attain your desires, which is entirely within your power. So, focus on what you can control. The person who possesses authority over what you desire or do not desire becomes your master. If you truly seek freedom, refrain from desiring or avoiding anything that falls under someone else's control. Otherwise, you are destined to become a slave.

Chapter 3 — Mastering Impressions

> *From lesson...*
>
> Focus on what you can control and avoid desires that are beyond your control. Do not be constrained by pursuing things that are under someone else's authority.

> **To action!**
>
> (1) Focus on what you can control: Instead of wishing for things that are out of your control, concentrate on the actions and decisions that you have power over.
> (2) Avoid wishing for immortality for your loved ones. Recognize that it is unrealistic and futile to desire eternal life for others. Understand that mortality is a natural part of life.
> (3) Do not try to possess what is not yours. Accept that you cannot control or own the lives of your children, spouse, or friends. Respect their autonomy and individuality.
> (4) Avoid having unrealistic expectations: Do not anticipate perfection or faultlessness from others, as if they were a slave-boy. Understand that everyone possesses flaws and imperfections.
> (5) Define vice as vice. Do not attempt to redefine or rationalize vices or negative behaviors as something different from their true nature. Acknowledge and address vices for what they really are.
> (6) Avoid desiring or avoiding things that are under someone else's control. Strive for true freedom by not yearning for or avoiding things that are dependent on someone else's authority or decisions.
> (7) Take responsibility for your own desires and actions. Recognize that you hold the power to shape both your desires and actions. Direct your focus and efforts towards achieving your personal goals.
> (8) Accept that disappointment is a part of life. Understand that you may encounter disappointments, but by focusing on what you can control, you can minimize the possibility of disappointment.

> **Approaching Life with Grace and Patience: The Path to Deserving Greatness**

15. Remember to approach life as you would at a fancy dinner party. When something comes your way, graciously partake in it. Do not hold on to it for too long; let it pass on. If something has not come to you yet, do not force it. Just wait until it is right in front of

you. This mentality should extend to how you treat children, your spouse, your job, and your finances. By living this way, eventually you will deserve the incredible opportunities that life has to offer. However, if you reject these presented opportunities and belittle them, not only will you miss the good things in life, but you will also miss the power and influence that come with them. Simply look at historical figures like Diogenes and Heraclitus, among others, who were revered for embodying this philosophy.

From lesson...

Approach life with grace and allow opportunities to flow through you, acknowledging their worth and embracing them wholeheartedly.

To action!

(1) Embrace opportunities: when something comes your way, graciously accept it, and seize a portion of it. Avoid clinging to it for too long and instead, allow it to pass on.
(2) Patience is key. If something has not come to you yet, there is no need to force it. Just wait until it presents itself right in front of you. It is important to practice patience in various aspects of life.
(3) Treat others with grace and apply the same approach of graciousness and acceptance when interacting with children, your spouse, colleagues, and even strangers. Treat everyone with kindness and respect.
(4) Value your job: Approach your job with the same mindset. Embrace the opportunities it presents and be open to new experiences and challenges. Do not reject or overlook professional opportunities that come your way.
(5) Manage your finances: Treat your money with the same grace as you would at a fancy dinner party. Be wise in your financial decisions, avoiding hoarding or excessively clinging to money. Instead, use it wisely and let it flow.
(6) Embrace the good things in life. By approaching life with a gracious and accepting mindset, you increase the likelihood of experiencing the wonderful things that life has to offer. Embrace these opportunities and fully appreciate them.

Chapter 3 — Mastering Impressions

(7) To avoid rejection and judgment, it is important to keep an open mind, rather than turning away opportunities or looking down on them. Instead, try to recognize their potential. By avoiding judgment and embracing the power and influence that come with accepting new experiences and opportunities, you can truly make the most of them.

(8) Learn from inspirational figures like Diogenes and Heraclitus, who were considered divine because they embraced life in this manner. Look at historical examples and draw lessons from their experiences, then apply their teachings to your own life.

(9) Cultivate a sense of deservingness by embracing the approach of gracefully accepting and letting opportunities pass by. Through practicing gratitude, self-improvement, and integrity, you can become deserving of the incredible things that life has to offer.

The Interpretation of Distress: Understanding Emotional Reactions

16. When you encounter someone in tears, whether it is due to their child going on a trip or losing their belongings, be cautious about assuming they are faced with external misfortunes. Instead, remind yourself that it is not the events alone that are causing this person distress, as it may not necessarily distress someone else, but rather their interpretation of those events. However, do not hesitate to offer words of sympathy or even shed a tear along with them if the situation warrants it, but ensure that it does not profoundly impact you.

From lesson...

When you encounter someone who is crying, remember that their interpretation of events, rather than the events themselves, is the underlying cause of their distress. Therefore, show sympathy without letting it deeply affect you.

To action!

(1) It is important to refrain from making assumptions regarding the reasons behind someone's tears.

(2) Remind yourself that it is the person's interpretation of events that is causing their distress, rather than the events themselves.

(3) If appropriate, offer words of sympathy or support to the person.

Chapter 3 — Mastering Impressions

(4) Show empathy by shedding a tear alongside the person if the situation calls for it.

(5) Be careful not to let the situation emotionally affect you deeply.

The Power of the Playwright: Embrace Your Assigned Role

17. Always remember that you are like an actor in a play, and the Playwright is the one who determines your character. If the Playwright wants the play to be brief, then it will be so. Should the Playwright cast you as a beggar, be sure to portray that role expertly. The same applies if you are assigned the role of a disabled person, an executive, or simply an ordinary individual. Your responsibility is to perform your assigned role exceptionally, but the selection of that role resides with someone else.

From lesson...

Remember that you are not in control of the role assigned to you, so accept it and give your best performance.

To action!

(1) Always keep in mind that your character is determined by someone else, just like being an actor in a play.

(2) Adapt and perform your assigned role with skill and excellence, irrespective of what it may be.

(3) Accept that the length of the play and the nature of your character are beyond your control.

(4) Embrace any role given to you, whether it portrays a beggar, executive, disabled person, or regular individual.

(5) Remember that your primary responsibility is to play your assigned role exceptionally well.

(6) Understand that the decision regarding your character belongs to the playwright or someone else.

The Power of Perception in Interpreting Signs and Omens

18. When a raven ominously caws, do not let it overwhelm you. Instead, take a moment to think clearly and say to yourself, "These signs are not meant for me, but perhaps for my physical well-being, material possessions, personal beliefs, loved ones, or relationships. However, I can choose to perceive any sign as favorable if I desire.

Chapter 3 — Mastering Impressions

Regardless of the outcome, I possess the ability to find something beneficial in it."

From lesson...

Do not let ominous signs overwhelm you; instead, choose to find something beneficial in them and perceive every sign as favorable if you desire to.

To action!

(1) Take a moment to pause and clear your mind when confronted with ominous signs or situations.

(2) Remind yourself that these signs may not be specifically meant for you but could be relevant to various aspects of your life, including physical well-being, material possessions, personal beliefs, loved ones, or relationships.

(3) Cultivate a mindset where you choose to see any sign as favorable if you so desire.

(4) Acknowledge that you possess the ability to discover something advantageous in every situation or result.

(5) Practice finding the unseen benefit or positive aspects in challenging circumstances.

(6) Take a moment to reflect on how the signs or situations you encounter may be related to your physical health, and then take the necessary actions to maintain or enhance it.

(7) Consider how the signs may be connected to your material possessions and take steps to protect and enhance them.

(8) Take a moment to pause and contemplate your personal beliefs and values. Consider how the signs align with these aspects of your life. Determine if any adjustments are necessary.

(9) Take into consideration how the signs may influence your relationships with your loved ones and try to enhance or cultivate those bonds.

(10) Embrace the idea that you can interpret signs and situations in a way that serves your well-being and brings positivity into your life.

Finding True Happiness and Freedom: The Power of Controlling What You Can

19. You can feel unstoppable if you avoid getting involved in any competition where you do not have control over the outcome. Be careful not to get carried away by external appearances when you see someone being praised, having power, or being highly regarded. Just because someone seems happy on the outside does not mean they truly are. If we understand that true happiness comes from within and is something we can control, then there is no room for envy or jealousy. You will not even desire to be a person of high social status like a judge or senator, but rather a free person. And the only way to achieve that freedom is by not placing importance on things we cannot control.

From lesson...

Focus on what you can control, avoid getting involved in competitions that are beyond your control, and find true happiness from within.

To action!

(1) Avoid entering competitions or participating in situations where you have no control over the outcome.
(2) Be cautious about being influenced by external appearances, such as praise, power, or high regard for others.
(3) It is important to understand that the outward happiness displayed by an individual may not necessarily reflect their true state of being.
(4) It is important to understand that genuine happiness originates from within oneself and that it is entirely under one's control.
(5) Release feelings of envy or jealousy by redirecting your focus towards regulating your own happiness.
(6) Value personal freedom over social status.
(7) Place importance on things that are within your control rather than those that are beyond your control.

Taking Control of Your Emotions: The Power of Perception

20. Always remember that it is not the person who insults or physically harms you that truly insults you, but rather, it is your own

Chapter 3 — Mastering Impressions

interpretation of their actions. So, when someone gets under your skin, recognize that it is your own perception that is causing you to feel irritated. Your first priority should be to not let external influences affect you too strongly. If you take a step back and give yourself some time to breathe, you will find it easier to regain control over your emotions.

> *From lesson...*
>
> Do not allow the actions of others to dictate your emotions. Instead, take a moment to pause, breathe, and regain ownership of your own perception.

To action!

(1) Practice self-awareness: Take the time to analyze your own thoughts and emotions when someone insults or harms you. Recognize that it is your own interpretation of their actions that is causing you to feel irritated.

(2) Developing a keen sense of self-worth is crucial. By building confidence and enhancing self-esteem, you can minimize the impact of external influences on your emotions. It is important to concentrate on your strengths and accomplishments to uphold a positive self-image.

(3) Cultivate resilience: Instead of letting insults or harm bring you down, develop the ability to bounce back from negative experiences. Build coping mechanisms, such as engaging in positive self-talk or seeking support from friends and loved ones, to help you overcome these challenges.

(4) Practice empathy: Try to understand the perspective of the person who insults or harms you. Doing so may help you recognize that their actions are often rooted in their own insecurities or problems, and not an accurate reflection of your self-worth.

(5) Take a step back: When confronted with a situation that upsets you, it is crucial to take a moment to pause and breathe. This simple act allows you to regain control over your emotions and effectively prevents any impulsive reactions that may only exacerbate the situation.

(6) Focus on what you can control. Instead of fixating on the actions of others, divert your attention to what you have the power to

influence – your own thoughts, emotions, and actions. Channel your energy towards engaging in positive and productive pursuits that bring you joy and fulfillment.

(7) Seek support: If you find it difficult to manage your emotions or overcome the impact of external influences, do not hesitate to seek support from professionals, such as therapists or counselors. They can provide guidance and strategies to help you navigate through challenging situations.

Embracing Death and Cultivating a Positive Mindset

21. Remember to keep death and all the things that seem awful in mind, especially death, every day. By doing so, you will never harbor negative or hopeless thoughts, nor will you develop excessive desires.

From lesson...

Always remember death; it will help you to cultivate gratitude, live in the present moment, and let go of unnecessary desires.

To action!

(1) Make it a daily practice to remind yourself of the inevitability of death.
(2) Whenever confronted with negative or hopeless thoughts, make a conscious effort to shift your focus towards recognizing death as a reminder of life's impermanence.
(3) Cultivate an attitude of acceptance towards things that may appear awful, acknowledging that they are a part of the human experience.
(4) Reflect on the concept of excessive desire and how it can lead to dissatisfaction or disappointment. Strive to maintain a balanced approach to your desires and avoid becoming excessively attached.
(5) Consider incorporating mindfulness or meditation techniques into your daily routine to help you stay grounded and focused on the uncertainties of life.
(6) Explore philosophical and spiritual perspectives on death and impermanence to deepen your understanding.
(7) Sharing these insights with others can initiate meaningful conversations about life, death, and the pursuit of contentment.

Chapter 3 — Mastering Impressions

(8) Find ways to actively appreciate and value the moments and experiences in life, recognizing that they are finite and may not be repeated.
(9) Journal or reflect on your thoughts and emotions regarding death, with the goal of developing a healthier perspective and relationship with it.
(10) Find inspiration in literature, art, or other avenues of expression that delve into the themes of mortality and the human condition.

The Challenges of Pursuing Philosophy

22. If you are interested in philosophy, be prepared to face ridicule. People may mock you and say things like, "Look who's suddenly turned into a philosopher," or "Where did you get that intellectual attitude from?" But do not let it discourage you. Stay true to your beliefs and hold on to what you think is right, just like someone who believes it is their destiny to do so. Remember, if you stick to your principles, those who used to laugh at you may eventually admire you. However, if you allow them to overpower you, you will end up being the one they laugh at.

From lesson...

Embrace philosophy despite any ridicule and stay resolute in your beliefs. In time, you will earn admiration for your principles.

To action!

(1) Be prepared to face ridicule if you are interested in philosophy.
(2) Do not let the mockery of others discourage you from pursuing philosophy.
(3) Stay true to your beliefs and principles in the face of criticism.
(4) Remember that it is important to hold on to what you believe is right, just like someone who passionately believes it is their destiny.
(5) Don't allow others to overpower you or dictate your beliefs.
(6) Stick to your principles, even if it means enduring ridicule.
(7) Understand that individuals who previously mocked you may eventually develop an admiration for your unwavering commitment and deeply held beliefs.

CHAPTER 4

— Mental Preparation

Epictetus discuss the importance of adopting the right mindset before engaging in tasks. This involves taking a holistic view, assessing our capabilities, and determining whether the task aligns with our values. By approaching tasks in a wise manner, we can avoid impulsive actions that we may later regret. To illustrate this concept, let us consider the preparation for a major sports event as a modern example.

Embracing Inner Wisdom: The Path to Living a Purposeful Life

23. If you ever find yourself trying to impress someone by solely focusing on external things, trust me, you are veering away from your life's purpose. Instead, find contentment in embodying a philosophical mindset in everything you do. And if you wish for others to perceive you as such, begin by proving it to yourself first. Once you accomplish that, you will instinctively radiate that image to others as well.

From lesson...

Focus on your internal growth and happiness instead of seeking validation from external sources.

To action!

(1) Take the time to ponder your life's purpose and pinpoint what genuinely brings you both meaning and fulfillment.

Chapter 4 — Mental Preparation

(2) Shift your focus from seeking validation externally to finding satisfaction internally.
(3) Embrace the role of a philosopher in everything you do by seeking wisdom, understanding, and introspection.
(4) Challenge yourself to live authentically by aligning your actions with your values and beliefs.
(5) Make personal growth and self-improvement a priority, constantly striving to deepen your understanding of both the world and yourself.
(6) Developing a keen sense of self-awareness is essential in recognizing both your strengths and areas for growth.
(7) Practice self-validation by finding joy and contentment in your own accomplishments and inner growth.
(8) Lead by example and inspire others through your actions and the way you live your life.
(9) Avoid seeking validation from others and instead, focus on cultivating a sense of self-fulfillment and self-worth.
(10) Stay true to yourself and trust that by being genuine and authentic, others will naturally perceive you as a philosopher.

Living a Life of Honor and Significance

24. Don't allow these thoughts to burden you: "I will live without honor and be insignificant everywhere." Because if the lack of honor is deemed negative, it is not as if someone else can make you bad, just as they cannot make you feel ashamed. It is not your responsibility to seek prestigious positions or be invited to fancy events, correct? So, how can it still be considered a lack of honor? And why would you be "insignificant everywhere" when you should only strive to be important in things that you can actually control, where you hold the privilege of being someone respected? But what about your friends? Will they be left without assistance? What does it mean to be "without help"? They will not receive slight change from you, and you will not make them citizens of a powerful empire. But who said that these are aspects under our control, rather than being in the hands of others? And who can give something to someone that they do not possess themselves? "Well then," a friend

may say, "acquire money so that we can have it too." If I can obtain money while preserving my self-respect, faithfulness, and integrity, then demonstrate how, and I will do it. However, if you want me to sacrifice the good things that are mine for you to acquire things that are not good, then you can observe for yourself how unjust and thoughtless you are being. And which do you truly value? Money or a loyal and self-respecting friend? Assist me in achieving the latter instead, and refrain from pushing me to engage in activities that will cause me to lose these qualities.

"But what about my country?" someone may inquire. "It will be left without assistance because of me." Once again, I ask, what kind of assistance are you referring to? It will not have extravagant buildings or luxurious baths that you provide. And what significance does that hold, anyway? It does not require shoes crafted by a blacksmith or weapons made by a cobbler; all it necessitates is for everyone to fulfill their own responsibilities. And if you were to introduce another loyal and self-respecting citizen to it, wouldn't that be beneficial? "Yes." Well then, you would not be of no use to it either. "But what role would I play in the State?" they question. Any role that allows you to maintain your loyalty and self-respect. Because if, in your eagerness to help the State, you forfeit those qualities, what purpose would you serve to it if you ultimately became shameless and untrustworthy?

From lesson...

Do not sacrifice your integrity and self-respect to seek external validation or try to please others.

To action!

(1) Reflect on the significance of honor and how it is unaffected by external factors or the opinions of others.
(2) Reconsider the pursuit of prestigious positions and invitations to fancy events, and instead, prioritize personal growth and making a difference in areas that are within our control.
(3) Understand that helping others does not necessarily mean providing material assistance or making them citizens of a powerful empire. Instead, focus on being a loyal and self-respecting friend.

Chapter 4 — Mental Preparation

(4) It is important to prioritize self-respect, faithfulness, and integrity in all our actions, even when it comes to pursuing wealth or success.
(5) If you are seeking guidance or examples on how to maintain self-respect, faithfulness, and integrity while pursuing financial success, there are various resources available. Look for inspiration from others who have successfully achieved both financial success and personal values. It can be helpful to seek the advice of mentors or role models who can offer insights and strategies for maintaining a strong moral compass in the pursuit of prosperity. Remember that it is possible to achieve financial success without compromising your principles. By learning from those who have found this balance, you can navigate your own path towards both financial security and personal fulfillment.
(6) Reject any requests or demands that would require you to compromise your personal qualities or values for the sake of others.
(7) It is important to understand that genuine assistance to one's country does not solely rely on providing material goods. It also encompasses individual contributions and the ability to attract loyal, self-respecting citizens to it.
(8) Embrace any role within the state that allows you to maintain fidelity and self-respect, instead of seeking positions that may compromise these qualities.
(9) It is important to consider the long-term consequences of sacrificing personal qualities and values in the pursuit of helping the state.
(10) Prioritize personal growth, self-improvement, and the maintenance of personal integrity over external recognition or material success.

The Importance of Managing Expectations and Pursuing Individual Paths

25. Have you ever felt jealous or disappointed when someone else was given more recognition, preferential treatment, or asked for advice instead of you? If these situations are positive, it is important to genuinely be happy for them. On the other hand, if they are negative, do not let it bother you because it means you did not have

to deal with those problems. Remember, if you do not follow the same path as others in pursuing things that are not under our control, you cannot expect to be treated equally.

Think about it this way: how can someone who doesn't constantly try to impress others expect to be treated the same way as someone who does? How can someone who does not do all the extra tasks expect to be rewarded the same way as the person who does? It would be unfair and unsatisfying if you refuse to put in the effort or pay the price for these things, yet still expect to have them handed to you for free.

Let us use the example of buying lettuce. The price for a head of lettuce, let us say, is a dollar. If someone decides to pay that dollar and gets their lettuce, while you choose not to pay and end up without lettuce, you cannot feel worse than the person who paid. They have their lettuce, and you have your dollar that you did not spend.

The same applies to life in general. If you have not been invited to a dinner party, it is because you did not give the host what they value, like admiration or attention. If you want to be invited, give them what they want, but only if it aligns with your own interests. However, if you expect to get all the benefits without making any sacrifices, you are being unreasonable and naive.

But fear not, there are always alternatives. By not attending the dinner party, you avoid having to praise someone you do not admire, and you do not have to deal with the rude behavior of their staff.

From lesson...

Be genuinely happy for the recognition that others receive, accept that different paths lead to different treatment, and do not expect rewards without putting in effort or making sacrifices.

To action!

(1) Be genuinely happy for others when they receive recognition or preferential treatment. Avoid any feelings of jealousy or disappointment, and instead, focus on celebrating their success.
(2) Understand that if you did not receive the same recognition or treatment, it may indicate that you were spared from the accompanying problems or difficulties.

Chapter 4 — Mental Preparation

(3) Recognize that if you do not follow the same path as others in pursuing things that are beyond your control, it is unrealistic to expect equal treatment.

(4) Take a moment to reflect on the effort you put into impressing others or going the extra mile. It is important to understand that those individuals who consistently put in more effort may receive greater rewards or recognition.

(5) It is important to acknowledge that expecting rewards or reaping benefits without making any sacrifices or putting in effort is both unfair and unrealistic.

(6) When you find yourself in situations where you feel excluded or overlooked, it is important to consider alternative options. Take the time to evaluate the potential benefits and drawbacks of participating and decide based on your own interests and values.

(7) If you choose not to participate in a situation, avoid dwelling on feelings of resentment or dissatisfaction. Instead, focus on the advantages of not having to compromise your values or deal with unfavorable circumstances.

Treat Yourself with Compassion and Understanding

26. To understand what nature intends for us, let us focus on the ways we are all alike. Think about it: when someone else's belongings break, such as a slave-boy breaking their drinking cup, we are quick to shrug it off and say, "Well, accidents happen." So, when our own cup shatters, we should react just as we would if it happened to someone else.

Now, let us apply this same mentality to more significant matters. When we hear that someone else's child or spouse has passed away, we understand that it is simply a part of life. We say, "That's the fate of humanity." But when it happens to us, we immediately cry out in anguish, thinking, "Oh no! Why me?" However, we should strive to remember how we empathize with others going through the same tragedy.

The message is clear: let us learn to treat ourselves with the same compassion and understanding that we show to others.

Chapter 4 — Mental Preparation

> *From lesson...*
> Treat yourself with the same compassion and understanding that you give to others.

> *To action!*
> (1) Recognize that accidents happen and shrug off small inconveniences or breakages, just as we would if they happened to someone else.
> (2) Apply the same mentality to more significant matters, such as the loss of a loved one, by understanding that it is a part of life and the destiny of humanity.
> (3) When faced with personal hardships or tragedies, it is important to avoid immediately reacting with anguish or self-pity.
> (4) Let us remember to empathize with others who may be going through similar tragedies or difficulties.
> (5) Learn to treat ourselves with the same compassion and understanding that we show to others.

The Significance of Evil in the World

27. Just like a sign is not put up to be ignored, the same goes for the presence of evil in the world.

> *From lesson...*
> Acknowledge and confront the reality of evil because ignoring it only enables its persistence and growth.

> *To action!*
> (1) Acknowledge and recognize the existence of evil: The first step is to consciously accept and acknowledge that evil exists in the world. It is important to understand that ignoring or denying its presence will not make it disappear.
> (2) Raise awareness: Take proactive steps to raise awareness about the existence of evil and its manifestations. This can be achieved through engaging in conversations, promoting education, sharing vital information, or actively supporting awareness campaigns.
> (3) Promote empathy and compassion: Evil often thrives in an environment that lacks empathy and compassion. It is crucial to actively promote these qualities within your personal and social

Chapter 4 — Mental Preparation

circles. You should encourage understanding, kindness, and support for others.

(4) Take a stand against injustice: Stand up against the injustices caused by evil actions. Whether it is advocating for human rights, combating systemic oppression, or fighting against discrimination, actively participate in actions that aim to bring about positive change.

(5) Report and address any wrongdoing: If you happen to encounter acts of evil, such as criminal activities or unethical behavior, be proactive and relay the information to the relevant authorities. By taking such action, you will be actively promoting accountability and working towards preventing any future harm.

(6) Support victims and survivors: Extend your support to those who have been affected by evil acts. This may involve providing emotional support, advocating for justice on their behalf, or helping them access relevant resources and services.

(7) Promote a safe environment by fostering inclusivity in both your personal and professional spaces. Aim to eradicate instances of harassment, abuse, and any kind of mistreatment. Cultivate a culture that prioritizes respect, equality, and fairness.

(8) Engage in acts of goodness: Counteract evil by actively participating in acts of goodness and kindness. Spread positivity and contribute positively to your community. Even small actions, such as volunteering, helping a stranger, or practicing random acts of kindness, can make a significant difference.

(9) Educate and empower future generations: Arm younger individuals with the knowledge and values essential for discerning and confronting malevolence. Instill in them critical thinking, empathy, and the significance of taking a stand against injustice.

(10) Support organizations that work against evil: Identify and support organizations and initiatives that are dedicated to combating evil and promoting positive change. This can be achieved through donations, volunteering, or raising awareness about their work.

(11) Remember that individual actions have the potential to collectively create a ripple effect and contribute to a more just and compassionate world.

Chapter 4 — Mental Preparation

> **The Vulnerability of Your Mind: Are You Giving It Away Too Easily?**

28. If someone randomly gave your body to anyone they met, you would be really annoyed. But here is the thing: you willingly give your mind to anyone who comes your way. And if they insult you, it is as if your mind goes into chaos and becomes all upset. Don't you feel embarrassed by that?

From lesson...

Guard and protect your mind from external influences by mastering the art of emotional resilience and preserving your inner peace.

To action!

(1) Take a moment to reflect on the significance of establishing boundaries with others. Begin by assessing the degree of trust and familiarity necessary for someone to gain access to your innermost thoughts and emotions.

(2) Practice self-awareness and mindfulness to recognize when someone's words or insults are impacting your mental wellbeing. Cultivate techniques, such as deep breathing, grounding exercises, or meditation, to regain control over your mind in these situations.

(3) Explore methods for building resilience and emotional strength, including therapy, self-help books, or support groups. These resources can help you develop the ability to remain composed and confident even when faced with criticism or insults.

(4) Consider implementing assertiveness training to learn effective ways of expressing your opinions, thoughts, and emotions without being overly affected by the judgments or insults of others.

(5) Take the time to reflect on your own self-worth and identity. Focus on developing a keen sense of self that is not heavily dependent on external validation or criticism.

(6) Engage in activities or hobbies that boost your self-esteem and reinforce your sense of self-worth, independent of others' opinions.

(7) Surround yourself with positive influences and supportive individuals who uplift and encourage you, thus minimizing the impact of negativity from others.

(8) Practice self-compassion and forgiveness. Understand that everyone makes mistakes, including yourself, and learn to release negative emotions or grudges that can lead to feelings of chaos or upset when confronted with insults.

(9) It is important to establish clear and assertive boundaries with individuals who consistently disrespect or insult you. Make your mental and emotional well-being a priority by limiting or completely ending contact with toxic individuals.

(10) Continuously work on personal growth and self-improvement to enhance your resilience and ability to handle emotional challenges gracefully. This can entail therapy, engaging in self-reflection, or participating in personal development activities.

Choosing Your Path: The Importance of Consideration and Commitment

29. When approaching any task, it is important to consider what comes before and after it before diving in. If you simply jump into something without thinking about the steps that follow, you may start off enthusiastic but end up giving up when faced with challenges. For instance, let us say you aspire to win an Olympic victory - that is a great goal! However, it is necessary to contemplate what you must do both before and after that. You will need to be disciplined, adhere to a strict diet, give up sweets, train consistently even when you do not feel like it, and follow a schedule irrespective of the weather. You cannot just consume whatever you want whenever you feel like it. You must devote yourself to your trainer in the same way you would to a doctor. Additionally, when it is time to compete, you must be prepared to face your opponents head-on, taking risks and accepting potential setbacks and injuries. Only after careful consideration of all these factors should you proceed if you still wish to pursue your goal. Otherwise, you will simply backtrack on your decision like a child. One moment they play wrestlers, the next they act as gladiators, blow trumpets, or perform in a play. In a similar vein, you have dabbled as an athlete, a gladiator, a speaker, and a philosopher, but you have not fully committed to anything. You merely imitate whatever catches your interest, without

Chapter 4 — Mental Preparation

thoughtful consideration or examination. If you desire to become a philosopher because you have witnessed someone like Euphrates speak (although, honestly, who can speak like him?), first consider if you are capable of handling it. Do you want to strive to be a pentathlon contender or a wrestler? Assess your physique - your arms, your thighs, your strength. Each person possesses their own natural talents. Can you alter your eating and drinking habits, as well as impulsive behavior? Can you commit to sleepless nights, hard work, solitude, and enduring disdain from others? Are you capable of enduring a consistently lower social status, position, and reputation? Ponder these challenges deeply and determine if the rewards of tranquility, freedom, and peace are sufficient for you. If not, then philosophy may not be the path for you. Do not emulate a child, constantly shifting roles - one moment a philosopher, the next a tax-gatherer, then a speaker, and later a servant of Caesar. These paths do not intertwine. You must choose who you aspire to be - good or bad. You must decide if you wish to work on self-improvement internally or externally. Either be a philosopher or be an ordinary person.

From lesson...

Before and after completing a task, it is important to consider the steps involved. Fully dedicate yourself to the process and then deliberately choose to work on self-improvement, whether it is internally or externally.

To action!

(1) Before beginning any task, it is important to take a moment to consider the steps that precede it and those that follow.
(2) Set clear goals for yourself, such as aiming for an Olympic victory. However, it is equally important to consider the actions and sacrifices that are necessary to attain these goals.
(3) Develop discipline and adhere to a strict diet and training regimen, even when faced with challenges or when lacking motivation.
(4) To maintain consistency, it is important to create a schedule and stick to it. This applies even when faced with external factors such as weather conditions or mood swings.

Chapter 4 — Mental Preparation

(5) Understand that to achieve your goals, you may need to give up certain indulgences or habits that do not contribute to your success.
(6) Devote yourself fully to your trainer or mentor, treating them with the same respect and commitment as you would a doctor.
(7) Be prepared to face difficulties and setbacks, including potential injuries, when the time comes to compete or achieve your goals.
(8) Before embarking on a particular path or role, it is crucial to critically assess whether you possess the essential qualities, talents, and level of commitment necessary for success.
(9) Consider the challenges and sacrifices associated with your desired path, such as changing eating habits, impulsive behaviors, sleepless nights, and isolation.
(10) Take a moment to ponder the possible benefits - tranquility, freedom, and peace - and carefully weigh them against the trials and sacrifices that might arise.
(11) Choose a path or role that aligns with your desires and abilities, whether it is as a philosopher or as an ordinary person.
(12) Avoid constantly changing roles or paths, and instead, commit to one and dedicate yourself to self-improvement both internally and externally.

Navigating Social Responsibilities: The Power of Relationships and Self-Reflection

30. Our responsibilities are determined by our social connections. For example, if someone is your father, you are expected to take care of them, prioritize their needs, and remain submissive even if they verbally attack or physically harm you. However, even if your father is not a good person, you still have a duty towards him simply because of your relationship. The same principle applies to other family members or people in your life who may treat you poorly.

If your brother mistreats you, it is important to maintain the relationship and focus on your own actions rather than his behavior. To align with your moral values and nature, do not get consumed by what he does but think about how you should respond. Remember, nobody can harm you without your permission. You only experience harm when you believe you have been harmed. By

Chapter 4 — Mental Preparation

adopting this mindset, you will better understand the responsibilities you have towards your neighbors, fellow citizens, and even your superiors by examining your social connections with them.

From lesson...

To gain a more profound understanding of your obligations towards others and to uphold your moral principles, it is imperative that you prioritize your own behavior and reactions. Moreover, it is vital to place emphasis on nurturing relationships, even with individuals who may mistreat you.

To action!

(1) Take care of your father and prioritize his needs, even if he verbally attacks or physically harms you.
(2) Remain submissive towards your father, regardless of his behavior.
(3) It is important to maintain your relationship with your brother, regardless of how he may mistreat you.
(4) Focus on your own actions and responses, rather than obsessing over the behavior of others.
(5) Always remember that nobody can harm you without your permission.
(6) Adopt the mindset that you only experience harm when you believe you have been harmed.
(7) To gain a better understanding of your responsibilities towards others, such as your neighbors, fellow citizens, and superiors, it is important to examine your social connections.

CHAPTER 5

— Social Roles and Duties

This chapter explores how we can fulfill our responsibilities and obligations in society while remaining virtuous. Whether we are being a good son, brother, parent, or citizen, he offers valuable advice that still applies to our lives today. Epictetus emphasizes the importance of staying true to our values rather than worrying about how others perceive us. He also encourages us to prioritize our relationship with a higher power and conduct ourselves wisely in social settings. Ultimately, our goal should be to maintain a strong moral compass in all aspects of our lives.

The Importance of Beliefs and Mindset in Devotion to the Gods

31. When it comes to showing respect and devotion to the gods, the most important aspect is having the correct beliefs about them. This involves recognizing their existence and understanding that they hold control over the world, ensuring fairness and justice. It also involves dedicating oneself to obeying them and accepting everything that occurs, believing it is all part of a greater plan guided by divine intelligence. Through behaving in this way, one will never blame the gods or accuse them of neglecting them.

However, achieving this mindset requires a change in perspective. It is essential to stop perceiving things beyond one's control as either good or evil and instead focus on what can be controlled. If external factors are categorized as good or bad, there will inevitably be blame and resentment towards those deemed responsible when things do not go as desired. Humans naturally tend to avoid and dislike things that appear harmful, while pursuing and admiring things that are beneficial. Consequently, if someone believes something is causing harm, they will not find pleasure in it or in the pain itself.

This is why family members can become enemies, like the brothers Polyneices and Eteocles, when they compete for something considered good, such as royal power. It is also why farmers, sailors, merchants, and individuals who have experienced the loss of loved ones may curse the gods, as their grievances are tied to their own interests. True devotion to the gods, therefore, is intricately connected to how we handle our desires and aversions. Those who are mindful of this are also practicing piety.

> *From lesson...*
>
> Shift your perspective, focus on what you can control, and embrace the divine plan to demonstrate respect and devotion to the gods.

> *To action!*
>
> (1) Develop the right beliefs about the gods, seeing them as both real entities and understanding their control over the world.
> (2) One should commit oneself to obeying the gods and accepting everything that happens as part of a divine plan.
> (3) Shift your perspective and stop labeling external factors as either good or bad.
> (4) Instead of resenting what cannot be controlled, it is better to focus on what can be controlled.
> (5) Avoid blaming and resenting those who are responsible for unfavorable outcomes.
> (6) Manage desires and aversions that are connected to personal interests and grievances.
> (7) Avoid blaming and accusing the gods of neglect.
> (8) Cultivate a mindset of piety by consciously managing your desires and aversions.

Chapter 5 — Social Roles and Duties

The Role of Divination and Reason in Decision-Making

32. When you turn to divination, remember that you are seeking answers, but you do not know what those answers will be. You are relying on the diviner to reveal them to you. However, if you consider yourself a philosopher, you already understand the situation before seeking guidance. If the matter at hand is beyond your control, then it is necessary to accept that the outcome will not be inherently good or evil.

So, when you approach the diviner, leave behind any desires or aversions, and do not tremble with fear. Instead, remind yourself that the outcome is indifferent and holds no power over you. Whatever it may be, you can find a way to make it work for your benefit, without anyone being able to stop you. Approach the gods with confidence, seeing them as wise counselors. And once you receive their guidance, remember who you sought advice from and the consequences of ignoring their counsel.

However, only turn to divination when you truly need answers that reason or other methods cannot provide. For example, when the outcome of a situation is uncertain, and you cannot find a logical solution. But in cases where the decision involves your loyalty to a friend or your duty to your country, do not rely on divination to tell you what to do. Even if the diviner warns of unfavorable signs or omens, you must use your own reasoning and stand by your friend, even if it means taking a risk or facing danger. Remember the lessons from Pythian Apollo, who banished the man who did not come to his friend's aid when he was being murdered.

From lesson...

Approach divination with confidence, accepting that the outcome holds no power over you, and rely on your own reasoning when it comes to questions of loyalty and duty.

To action!

(1) When seeking divination, approach with an open mind and let go of any desires or aversions.

(2) Remind yourself that the outcome of divination is irrelevant and holds no power over you.

(3) Find a way to harness the divined outcome to your advantage, all the while ensuring that no one can impede your progress.
(4) Approach the gods with confidence, viewing them as wise counselors.
(5) Remember who you sought advice from and consider the consequences of disregarding their guidance.
(6) Only resort to divination when reason or other methods are unable to provide the answers you need.
(7) Use divination in situations where the outcome is uncertain and logical solutions are elusive.
(8) Do not depend on divination when it comes to making decisions regarding your allegiance to a friend or your duty towards your country.
(9) When faced with situations that test your loyalty or sense of duty, rely on your own judgment, and remain steadfast in supporting your friend, even if it means facing potential risks or dangers.
(10) Learn from the lessons of Pythian Apollo, who banished a man for failing to assist his friend in a time of need.

Setting a Strong and Noble Character: Guidelines for Engaging with Others

33. Set a clear and consistent character for yourself from the start, whether you are alone or with others. Speak sparingly, only when necessary, and keep your remarks concise. However, when you do speak, ensure that it is about topics of substance, rather than the usual subjects like sports or food. And avoid gossiping about other people, whether it is criticizing or praising them. Instead, try to steer the conversation towards more meaningful subjects. However, if you find yourself alone with strangers, it is best to remain silent.

Do not laugh excessively or at everything. If possible, avoid taking oaths altogether. But if you cannot, limit them as much as possible based on the situation.

Stay away from parties thrown by people who do not understand or appreciate philosophy. But if you must attend, make sure you do not get caught up in their behavior. Remember, if you spend time together with someone who is messy, you are likely to get dirty too, regardless of your own cleanliness.

When it comes to material possessions, only take what you truly need for survival – food, drink, clothing, shelter, and essential household items. Cut out anything that is just for show or unnecessary luxury.

Maintain purity in your relationships before marriage, and if you do engage in activities, make sure they are lawful. However, do not be judgmental or offensive towards those who choose differently, and avoid mentioning your personal choices too frequently.

If someone tells you that others are speaking ill of you, do not feel the need to defend yourself. Instead, acknowledge their comments and say there are many more faults they do not know about. Most of the time, you do not need to attend public shows. But if you do, focus on yourself, and accept whatever outcome happens. Avoid shouting, laughing at others, or getting too worked up. And after the show, do not dwell on it unless it contributes to your personal growth. Talking excessively about it implies you were overly impressed.

Be selective about attending public readings, and when you do go, maintain your dignity without becoming unpleasant. When meeting someone important, ask yourself what great philosophers like Socrates or Zeno would do in that situation. This will guide you on how to best handle it. Similarly, when visiting someone powerful, prepare yourself for the possibility of being turned away or ignored. If you still decide to go, accept the outcome without complaining. Do not let yourself think it was not worth the effort, as that is the mindset of someone who gets upset over external circumstances.

In conversations, avoid bragging about your own achievements or adventures excessively, as others may not find them as interesting as you do. Also, be cautious about making jokes, as they can easily become crude and lessen the respect others have for you. It is important to refrain from using vulgar language as well. If someone crosses that line, if appropriate, politely address their behavior. Otherwise, show your disapproval through your silence, blushing, or a stern expression.

Chapter 5 — Social Roles and Duties

> **From lesson...**
>
> To maintain a clear and consistent character, it is important to speak wisely and engage in meaningful conversations. It is crucial to avoid gossip and to limit excessive laughter and oaths as well. Additionally, staying away from negative influences and prioritizing essential possessions are also important.
>
> Upholding purity in relationships is vital, as is choosing not to defend oneself against rumors. Instead, it is better to focus on personal growth and handle important situations with dignity. Accepting outcomes without complaining is a sign of emotional maturity, as is refraining from bragging or making crude jokes. Lastly, showing disapproval of vulgar language is a demonstration of respect.

> **To action!**
>
> (1) Set a clear and consistent character for yourself, both when you are alone and when you are with others.
>
> (2) Speak sparingly, only when necessary, and ensure that your remarks are concise.
>
> (3) Discuss meaningful topics, avoiding conversations about sports or food.
>
> (4) Avoid engaging in gossip or passing judgment on others during conversations.
>
> (5) Guide the conversation towards more meaningful topics.
>
> (6) If you ever find yourself alone with strangers, it is advisable to remain silent.
>
> (7) Avoid laughing excessively or laughing at everything.
>
> (8) It is advisable to limit or even avoid taking oaths, depending on the situation.
>
> (9) Avoid attending parties hosted by individuals who do not value philosophy.
>
> (10) If you attend such parties, do not get caught up in their behavior.
>
> (11) Be mindful of the company you keep, as associating with untidy individuals can have an influence on your own cleanliness.
>
> (12) Take only what you genuinely need for survival in terms of material possessions.

Chapter 5 — Social Roles and Duties

(13) Eliminate anything that is unnecessary or solely for display purposes.

(14) It is essential to maintain purity in relationships before marriage and engage in lawful activities.

(15) Do not be judgmental or offensive towards others who make different choices.

(16) It is advisable to refrain from frequently making references to personal choices.

(17) There is no need to feel compelled to defend yourself when others speak ill of you. Instead, simply acknowledge their comments and subtly remind them that there are other faults they may not be aware of.

(18) Avoid attending public shows unless necessary. Instead, focus on yourself and accept the outcome.

(19) Refrain from shouting, laughing at others, or becoming overly excited during public performances.

(20) After a performance, it is best to avoid dwelling on it unless it adds value to your personal development.

(21) To maintain your dignity without becoming unpleasant, it is important to be selective when attending public readings.

(22) Imagine how great philosophers would handle meeting someone important.

(23) Be prepared for the potentiality of being turned away or disregarded when visiting someone in a position of power.

(24) Accept the outcome without complaining when visiting someone powerful.

(25) It is advisable to refrain from excessive bragging about achievements or adventures during conversations.

(26) Be cautious when making jokes, as they have the potential to become crude and diminish the respect others have for you.

(27) Refrain from using vulgar language and address such behavior politely if it is appropriate.

(28) Demonstrate disapproval by remaining silent, blushing, or adopting a stern expression when someone crosses the line with their behavior.

Chapter 5 — Social Roles and Duties

Navigating Pleasure: Finding Balance and Resisting Temptation

34. When you come across something that brings you pleasure, exercise caution. Do not allow yourself to be carried away by it as with any other distraction. Instead, take a moment to pause and reflect on it. Consider two different time frames: the first being when you are actually enjoying the pleasure, and the second after it has passed, when you are left feeling regretful and disappointed. Compare these two periods of time with the satisfaction and contentment you will experience if you resist succumbing to the pleasure.

However, if you believe the right moment has arrived to indulge in this pleasure, be careful not to let its allure overpower you. Instead, remind yourself of how much better it feels to overcome temptation and achieve victory over it.

From lesson...

Be cautious and take a moment to consider the consequences of indulgence. Compare temporary pleasure with long-lasting fulfillment and always remember the satisfaction that arises from resisting temptation and achieving triumph.

To action!

(1) Practice mindfulness: When you encounter something that brings you joy, take a moment to consciously pause and appreciate it. Do not allow yourself to be carried away without being fully present in the moment.

(2) Reflect on past experiences: Take the time to reflect on instances when you have given in to immediate pleasure and later felt regret or disappointment. Compare this with moments when you resisted temptation and experienced satisfaction and contentment. Use these reflections as motivation to resist the impulsive urge to give in to pleasure.

(3) Consider the long-term consequences: Before giving in to a pleasurable experience, take a moment to reflect on the potential negative outcomes or consequences that could occur afterward. Assess whether the short-lived pleasure is utterly worth the possible feelings of regret or disappointment that may ensue.

(4) Focus on delayed gratification: Instead of seeking immediate pleasure, remind yourself of the greater satisfaction and contentment that can come from resisting temptation. Cultivate a mindset that values long-term fulfillment over short-lived pleasure.

(5) Build resilience against allure: Recognize the allure and temptation that pleasure may hold and be mindful not to let it overpower your ability to resist. Remind yourself of the strength and victory that come from overcoming temptation.

(6) Develop self-discipline: Train yourself to resist giving in to immediate pleasure by practicing self-discipline in other areas of your life. Look for opportunities to exercise self-control and delay gratification, as this will enhance your ability to resist pleasure when necessary.

(7) Seek support and accountability: Share your goals and struggles with trusted friends or loved ones who can provide support and hold you accountable. Having someone to talk to or check in with can help you stay focused on resisting temptations and achieving long-term satisfaction.

(8) Create a plan: If you believe the right moment has come to indulge in a particular pleasure, it is important to create a plan beforehand. By setting boundaries and limits, you can ensure that you do not get carried away. Having a clear plan in place will help you make more thoughtful and intentional decisions when faced with temptation.

(9) Celebrate your victories: Acknowledge and celebrate the moments when you successfully resist immediate pleasure. Rewarding yourself for overcoming temptations can strengthen the positive feelings of satisfaction and contentment that come with delayed gratification.

(10) Practice self-reflection: Regularly reflect on your progress in resisting impulsive pleasures and evaluate any changes or improvements in your mindset and behavior. Use this self-reflection to continuously refine and strengthen your ability to resist distractions and prioritize long-term fulfillment.

Chapter 5 — Social Roles and Duties

Embrace Your Beliefs and Overcome Judgement

35. When you are determined to do something that you believe is right, do not worry about others judging you. Do not hide your actions, even if most people might disapprove. However, if what you are doing is wrong, then it is best to avoid it altogether. But if it is indeed the right thing to do, why should you be afraid of those who will criticize you unfairly?

From lesson...

Stay true to your beliefs and actions, regardless of the judgement of others, as long as you know you are doing what is right.

To action!

(1) Take time to reflect on your actions and beliefs, making sure they are in line with your values and morals.
(2) Have confidence in your decisions and have faith in your own judgement, irrespective of what others may think.
(3) Seek constructive criticism from trusted individuals who can provide valuable insights and perspectives.
(4) Find support from like-minded individuals or communities that share your belief in the righteousness of your actions.
(5) Educate yourself about the potential consequences or risks associated with your decision and take the necessary precautions.
(6) Stand up for what you believe in, even in the face of unfair criticism or judgement.
(7) Stay receptive to constructive feedback and be willing to reassess your actions if added information or perspectives come to light.
(8) Strive to communicate effectively and respectfully with others, even if they happen to disapprove of your choices.
(9) Advocate for your beliefs and inspire others to take action if they, too, believe in the righteousness of the cause.
(10) Learn from past experiences, both successes and failures, to continually enhance and refine your approach to accomplishing what you deem as right.

Chapter 5 — Social Roles and Duties

> **Finding Balance Between Self-Care and Social Context at the Dinner Table**

36. Imagine this: you are sitting at a dinner table with someone, both enjoying a delicious meal. Now, let us say you have the opportunity to take a bigger portion of the food for yourself. On one hand, it seems like a great idea because it would satisfy your hunger and benefit your body. But on the other hand, it might negatively impact the atmosphere and social connection between you and your dining partner.

Just like how the statements "It is day" and "It is night" have different meanings when considered separately but make no sense when combined, this situation presents a similar dilemma. While prioritizing your physical needs is important, it is equally crucial to consider the impact on the relationship and social dynamics at play.

So next time you find yourself sharing a meal with someone, remember not only to think about what is best for your own body but also to maintain respect for your host and preserve the harmonious atmosphere. It is all about finding that balance between taking care of yourself and being mindful of the social context.

From lesson...

When sharing a meal with someone, it is important to consider the impact it may have on your social connection and to maintain respect. Finding a balance between taking care of yourself and being mindful of the social context is crucial.

To action!

(1) Prioritizing your physical needs is crucial. Pay close attention to your hunger and ensure that you are fully satisfied during the meal.
(2) Consider the impact on your relationship: Reflect on how taking a larger portion might influence the social connection and atmosphere between you and your dining partner.
(3) Maintain respect for your host by showing appreciation for the meal. Be mindful of your actions and consider the efforts of your host in preparing the food.

Chapter 5 — Social Roles and Duties

(4) To maintain the harmonious atmosphere, it is important to avoid any actions that could disturb the positive ambiance or create tension during the meal.

(5) Find a balance: Strive to strike a compromise between attending to your own needs and being mindful of the social context.

The Consequences of Taking on Unattainable Roles

37. If you take on a role that is beyond your abilities, you will not only embarrass yourself in that role but also neglect the role in which you could have succeeded.

From lesson...

Choose roles that align with your abilities to avoid embarrassment and maximize your potential for success.

To action!

(1) Before accepting a role, it is crucial to evaluate both your abilities and limitations. Take the time to assess your skills, knowledge, and experience to determine whether you have the capability to fulfill the responsibilities that come with the role.

(2) Seek feedback and advice from trusted individuals or mentors who can provide objective insights into your abilities, considering their perspectives and taking their suggestions into account before committing to a role.

(3) Focus on your strengths and identify roles that align with your skill set. By selecting positions that fall within your capabilities, you will be able to excel and make a significant contribution.

(4) Develop and enhance your skills to prepare yourself for roles that may require additional expertise. Take courses, attend workshops, or actively seek out opportunities for professional growth to expand your abilities.

(5) To excel in all your roles without neglecting any of them, it is important to prioritize your commitments and avoid taking on too many responsibilities at once. By effectively managing your workload, you can allocate sufficient time and effort to each task.

(6) Continuously assess your performance in the roles you have assumed. Regularly evaluate whether you are meeting expectations and delivering satisfactory results. If you find yourself struggling or

unable to perform effectively, consider reevaluating your commitments.

(7) Be open to delegation and collaboration. If you realize that a particular role is beyond your abilities or that you may not be able to give it your best, consider delegating certain tasks or seeking support from others who are better suited to those responsibilities.

(8) It is important to communicate openly and honestly with the individuals involved in the roles you have taken on. If you find yourself struggling or in need of stepping back, it is crucial to initiate a conversation with the relevant parties, discussing potential solutions or alternative arrangements.

(9) Learn from any unsuccessful attempts at taking on roles beyond your abilities. Reflect on the experience, identify the areas where you may have fallen short, and use those insights to make better decisions in the future.

(10) Embrace self-awareness and humility, recognizing and accepting your limitations. It is important to acknowledge that not every role will be suitable for you. By staying realistic and grounded, you can ensure that you focus your efforts on roles where you have the highest chances of succeeding.

Protecting Your Inner Guidance: A Key to Well-Being and Safe Navigation

38. Just as you are cautious about not stepping on a nail or spraining your ankle while walking, it is equally important to be mindful of protecting your inner guidance. By following this principle in every action, you will enhance your overall well-being and safeguard yourself from unnecessary trouble.

From lesson...

Protect your inner guidance and enhance your well-being by practicing mindfulness in every action.

To action!

(1) Pay attention to your intuition. Practice tuning into your inner guidance and trust the gut feelings or instincts that arise in various situations.

(2) Reflect on your decisions: Before taking any action, pause for a moment and consider if it aligns with your inner guidance and values.
(3) Set boundaries: Learn to say no to things that do not align with your inner guidance and prioritize activities and relationships that promote your well-being.
(4) Practice self-care: Make sure to dedicate time to nurture yourself physically, mentally, emotionally, and spiritually. This can entail engaging in activities like exercising, meditating, journaling, or immersing yourself in nature.
(5) Surround yourself with positive influences: Evaluate the people and environments with which you regularly interact and strive to surround yourself with individuals who uplift and inspire you.
(6) Make it a point to seek solitude: carve out regular time for yourself to reflect, recharge, and connect with your inner guidance. You can achieve this through activities such as taking solitude walks, practicing silent meditation, or creating a designated quiet space at home.
(7) Trust your own judgment: Have faith in your ability to make sound decisions based on your inner guidance, even if they differ from the opinions or expectations of others.
(8) Practice mindfulness: Cultivate present moment awareness and bring conscious attention to your thoughts, feelings, and actions. This can help you stay connected to your inner guidance and make choices that align with your well-being.
(9) Learn from past experiences: Reflect on past situations in which you followed or ignored your inner guidance. Utilize these experiences as valuable learning opportunities to refine your ability to trust and safeguard your inner guidance in the future.
(10) If you find it challenging to connect with or protect your inner guidance, consider seeking support and guidance from a trusted friend, mentor, or therapist who can offer valuable insights and support.

Proportional Possessions: Maintaining Balance and Avoiding Excess

39. Every person should have possessions that are in proportion to their body, much like how a shoe size is determined by the size of

the foot. Following this principle ensures that you have the right number of possessions. However, if you exceed this measure, you will undoubtedly face difficulties and experience a metaphorical downfall. The same concept applies to shoes - if your shoe size is too big, you may start with fancy shoes, but eventually move on to extravagant ones, with no end in sight once you surpass the appropriate size.

From lesson...

Make sure that your belongings are appropriate for your body size; otherwise, you will face the consequences of excessive indulgence.

To action!

(1) Evaluate the proportion between the size of your body and your possessions. Conduct an inventory of your belongings and assess if they align with your needs and lifestyle, considering aspects like space, functionality, and practicality.

(2) Identify any possessions that exceed the appropriate proportion. Look for items that serve no practical purpose or are only used occasionally. Consider downsizing or letting go of these excess belongings that take up valuable space and resources.

(3) When making new purchases, prioritize functionality and practicality over extravagance and excess. Make sure that any new items you acquire serve a purpose and align with your needs instead of being lured by unnecessary luxury or status symbols.

(4) To maintain a balanced and proportional collection, it is important to regularly declutter your possessions. Schedule decluttering sessions throughout the year to periodically reassess your belongings and eliminate any unnecessary items.

(5) Practice mindful consumption and avoid excessive accumulation. Instead of constantly seeking to acquire more possessions, focus on investing in quality items that will truly enhance your life and align with your needs in the appropriate proportion.

(6) When it comes to possessions, consider sustainable options. Look for eco-friendly products and materials that have a lower impact on the environment. Choose durable items that will last longer, reducing the need for frequent replacements or upgrades.

(7) Remember that possessions do not define your worth or success. Avoid falling into the trap of acquiring more and more in an attempt to find happiness or validation. Instead, focus on experiences, relationships, and personal growth as the true sources of fulfillment.

(8) Share and repurpose possessions whenever possible. Rather than hoarding items that are no longer needed, consider donating or selling them to others who may benefit from them. Seek opportunities to repurpose or recycle materials to minimize waste and contribute to a more sustainable lifestyle.

(9) Educate yourself about minimalism and intentional living by delving into resources and guides. Discover how to thrive with fewer possessions, prioritizing quality over quantity. Draw inspiration from individuals who have wholeheartedly embraced the minimalist lifestyle and adapt their principles to your own belongings.

(10) Regularly reflect on the impact that your possessions have on your life. Take moments to evaluate whether your belongings are truly bringing you joy, fulfillment, and convenience, or if they are becoming burdensome and hindering your overall well-being. Adjust accordingly to maintain a healthy and proportional relationship with your possessions.

CHAPTER 6

— Mental Fortitude and Appropriate Actions

In this chapter, Epictetus offers insightful advice on making the right choices in our lives. He warns against acting on impulsive desires, emphasizes the importance of balance, and provides guidance on our behavior regarding sexuality and avoiding excess. According to Epictetus, it is crucial for us to act purposefully and in moderation, ensuring that our core values align with the natural flow of things. By doing so, we can experience genuine inner freedom.

Empowering Young Women: Moving Beyond Appearance

40. As soon as girls turn fourteen, they are often referred to as "ladies" by men. Consequently, they come to the realization that their value is largely determined by their connections with men. As a result, they start placing significant importance on their appearance, hoping that it will garner them validation and acknowledgment. It is crucial for us to make them realize that they are deserving of respect not just for their physical appearance, but also for their humility and self-esteem.

From lesson...

Empower women by reminding them that their worth is not solely based on their appearance but also on their intelligence, strength, and self-worth.

Chapter 6 — Mental Fortitude and Appropriate Actions

To action!

(1) Educate young women about the significance of valuing themselves beyond their physical appearance. Design programs or workshops that prioritize the development of self-esteem, self-worth, and the cultivation of other skills and talents that extend beyond mere looks.

(2) Encourage a diverse range of role models by promoting the visibility of successful women in various fields. Emphasize their accomplishments, intelligence, and character rather than solely focusing on their physical attributes.

(3) Foster a supportive environment by creating safe spaces where young women can openly discuss their insecurities, challenges, and the societal pressures they may face. Offer counseling services or support groups aimed at helping them develop healthy coping mechanisms and cultivate a positive body image.

(4) Teach critical thinking skills: Provide educational materials and workshops to help young women develop their abilities to question and challenge societal norms and expectations placed upon them. Encourage them to think critically about the messages they receive from media, society, and even their own peers.

(5) Promote self-expression and individuality by encouraging young women to explore their interests and hobbies beyond traditional gender roles. Provide opportunities for them to participate in activities that allow them to express their unique identities and strengths.

(6) Engage men in the conversation: Educate boys and men on the importance of respecting women for more than just their looks. Encourage open dialogues about gender equality and challenge harmful stereotypes and expectations.

(7) Provide mentorship opportunities by establishing mentorship programs where successful women can guide and inspire young women to pursue their goals. Emphasize the importance of personal growth, achievements, and self-respect in these programs.

(8) Collaborate with schools and education systems: Work with schools to integrate comprehensive sex education programs that emphasize healthy relationships, consent, and self-esteem.

Chapter 6 — Mental Fortitude and Appropriate Actions

Additionally, provide training for teachers on how to address harmful gender stereotypes and promote equal treatment among students.

(9) Be an advocate for media literacy by encouraging media outlets to portray women in diverse and empowering ways. This involves promoting realistic body images and showcasing their achievements, rather than solely focusing on their appearance. Additionally, supporting initiatives that challenge objectification and promote positive representation of women is vital.

(10) Encourage community involvement: Promote opportunities for young women to engage in community service, advocacy, and leadership roles. This will help build their confidence, enable them to make a tangible impact, and reinforce the idea that their worth extends beyond their physical appearance.

Balancing Physical and Mental Well-being

41. It is a sign of lacking talent to excessively focus on your physical self, such as engaging in excessive workouts, overeating, heavy drinking, or spending excessive time in the bathroom. These activities should only play a minor role in your life, whereas your main priority should be the development of your mind and intellect.

From lesson...

Make developing your mind and intellect your primary focus, rather than becoming consumed by excessive physical activities or unhealthy habits.

To action!

(1) Do mental exercise a priority by dedicating daily time to activities such as reading, solving puzzles, or engaging in challenging conversations. These activities will help you develop your mind and intellect.

(2) Create a well-balanced workout routine: Rather than overdoing it with excessive workouts, strive for a moderate and consistent exercise regimen that incorporates both cardiovascular and strength training exercises.

(3) Practice mindful eating: Avoid overeating by maintaining awareness of portion sizes and paying attention to your body's hunger

Chapter 6 — Mental Fortitude and Appropriate Actions

and satiety signals. Make nourishing your body with wholesome foods your main focus.

(4) Limit alcohol consumption: Practice moderation when it comes to drinking alcohol, choosing to indulge in social occasions or extraordinary events rather than engaging in heavy drinking regularly.

(5) Allocate your time efficiently: Minimize unnecessary time spent in the bathroom by ensuring regular bowel movements through a balanced diet, proper hydration, and maintaining a healthy lifestyle.

(6) To enhance personal growth, make it a priority to invest time in personal development. This can be achieved through engaging in activities such as reading self-help books, participating in workshops or seminars, or acquiring new skills.

(7) Cultivate healthy habits by incorporating mindfulness practices, such as meditation or journaling, to enhance self-awareness and maintain a balanced approach to life.

(8) To seek intellectual stimulation, engage in activities such as joining book clubs, attending lectures, or participating in group discussions. These pursuits will help broaden your knowledge and enhance your critical thinking abilities.

(9) Engage in regular self-reflection to ensure that your actions are aligned with your values, goals, and aspirations, promoting personal growth and intellectual development.

(10) Balance physical and mental well-being by recognizing that both physical health and mental and intellectual growth are equally important. This holistic approach to personal improvement ensures that you give equal attention to both aspects of your well-being.

Navigating Negative Interactions: Understanding Others' Perspectives

42. When someone mistreats you or says negative things about you, remember that they do so because they believe it is their duty. From their perspective, they cannot align with what you believe is right, but with what they believe is right. This means that if they have a distorted understanding of things, they are actually deceiving themselves. So, when someone insults you, try to be understanding. Remind yourself that they simply see things differently.

Chapter 6 — Mental Fortitude and Appropriate Actions

> *From lesson...*
>
> Do not let negative words and mistreatment from others determine your worth or undermine your understanding. Keep in mind that their perspective is inherently limited and flawed. Therefore, constantly strive to maintain compassion and remain authentic to yourself.

> *To action!*

(1) Practice empathy: Instead of reacting with anger or resentment when someone mistreats or insults you, try to put yourself in their shoes and understand their perspective. Remember that they may be acting based on their own beliefs and values.

(2) Avoid taking it personally. Instead of internalizing negative comments or mistreatment, remind yourself that they are more about the other person's perception and beliefs, rather than a reflection of your worth or abilities.

(3) Focus on self-reflection: Use these experiences as an opportunity for personal growth and self-improvement. Consider whether there is any validity to the criticisms or negative comments and focus on areas that you may need to develop.

(4) Foster self-confidence by reminding yourself of your own worth and values. It is important to build a keen sense of self-assurance, so that negative comments or mistreatment from others do not negatively impact your self-esteem.

(5) Choose your battles wisely: not every insult or negative comment requires a response or reaction. Learn to discern when it is necessary to address the issue and when it is better to simply let it go.

(6) Seek support: Surround yourself with a supportive network of friends, family, or mentors who can provide encouragement and help you navigate challenging situations. Share your experiences with them and ask for advice on how to handle such situations positively.

(7) Practice forgiveness: Understand that people may make mistakes and act out of their own shortcomings. Make an effort to be forgiving and let go of any resentment or grudges you may hold towards those who mistreat or insult you.

(8) Educate and communicate: If appropriate, engage in a calm and respectful conversation to help the other person understand your

Chapter 6 — Mental Fortitude and Appropriate Actions

perspective and challenge their distorted beliefs. This approach can potentially lead to a better understanding and resolution of any conflicts.

(9) Set boundaries: If mistreatment or insults become recurring or abusive, it is vital to establish clear boundaries and prioritize your well-being. Determine what you are unwilling to tolerate and confidently communicate these boundaries to the other person.

(10) Practice self-care: Engage in activities that promote your emotional and mental well-being. This can include exercising, practicing mindfulness or meditation, pursuing hobbies, or seeking professional help if necessary. Taking care of yourself will enable you to build resilience and effectively cope with any negative experiences.

Approaching Conflict with Compassion: Handling Difficult Situations with Family

43. Every situation can be approached in two ways: one that is helpful and one that is not. When your brother mistreats you, it is important not to solely focus on the wrongdoing itself, as that is not the most effective way to handle the situation. Instead, try considering the fact that he is your brother, someone you grew up with. By adopting this approach, you will be dealing with the matter in the way it should be handled.

From lesson...

Focus on the positive aspects of your relationship and handle conflicts with your brother in a considerate and understanding manner.

To action!

(1) Recognize that every situation can be approached in two ways - a helpful and an unhelpful way.

(2) When confronted with mistreatment from your brother, it is best to avoid solely fixating on the wrongdoing itself.

(3) Take into consideration the relationship and history you have with your brother, acknowledging the fact that you both grew up together.

(4) Approach the situation with the intention of handling it correctly.

(5) Shift your mindset to focus on finding a solution or resolution instead of dwelling on the negative aspects of mistreatment.

(6) To maintain a healthy relationship with your brother, it is crucial to have open communication. This allows you to gain insight into his perspective and effectively resolve any misunderstandings that may arise.

(7) Practice empathy and try to see the situation from your brother's perspective, considering any possible underlying reasons for his actions.

(8) The key is to seek common ground and actively work towards rebuilding a positive relationship with your brother.

(9) Engage in constructive conversations or mediation to address any conflicts or issues between you and your brother.

(10) If the mistreatment continues or worsens, it may be worth considering seeking professional help or guidance, such as family counseling.

Making Sense of Statements: Moving Beyond Surface Comparisons

44. Some statements simply do not make sense. For instance, claiming "I have more money than you, so I'm superior" or "I speak better than you, so I'm better than you." These statements just do not hold true. However, it does make more sense to say, "I have more money than you, so my possessions are of higher quality than yours" or "I speak better than you, so my way of expressing myself is more refined." But here is the catch: you are not defined by your belongings or your manner of speech. You are so much more than that.

From lesson...

Do not measure your worth by comparing possessions or abilities because you are more than just what you have and how you speak.

To action!

(1) Take a moment to reflect on the statements you make about yourself and others. Are they predominantly centered around material possessions or superficial qualities? Try to refocus your attention towards more meaningful aspects of your identity.

Chapter 6 — Mental Fortitude and Appropriate Actions

(2) Challenge the notion that having more money or better speaking abilities automatically makes someone superior. Recognize and appreciate the diversity in skills, qualities, and strengths that individuals possess.

(3) Emphasize the value of personal growth and development and actively seek out opportunities to enhance your skills, knowledge, and understanding. Instead of comparing yourself to others, focus on improving yourself.

(4) Promote empathy and understanding by embracing the concept that each individual is multifaceted and cannot be easily characterized solely based on material possessions or speaking abilities.

(5) Engage in self-reflection to identify and nurture the qualities and traits that hold true importance to you. Direct your attention towards personal development and striving to become the finest version of yourself, rather than constantly comparing yourself to others.

(6) Encourage and appreciate the unique strengths and qualities in others, recognizing that their worth is not solely determined by material wealth or linguistic abilities.

(7) Practice mindful communication, instead of ranking or comparing yourself to others, aim to connect and understand different perspectives, fostering a more inclusive and compassionate dialogue.

(8) Engage in activities and cultivate relationships that foster personal growth, empathy, and authenticity. Surround yourself with individuals who genuinely appreciate and value you for who you truly are, going beyond surface-level markers of success.

Understanding Motives: The Importance of Avoiding Judgement

45. If someone rushes through their bathing routine, do not judge them as being bad at it; instead, recognize their eagerness. Similarly, if someone enjoys a lot of wine, do not label them as a bad drinker, but rather acknowledge their preference for indulging. Before passing any judgements, it is important to consider the motives behind their actions. How can you determine if something is truly bad without understanding their reasoning? By keeping an open mind and

Chapter 6 — Mental Fortitude and Appropriate Actions

considering various perspectives, you can avoid being swayed by mere appearances and make more informed decisions.

From lesson...

Before making any judgements, it is important to recognize individuals' motives and carefully consider multiple perspectives.

To action!

(1) Do not jump to conclusions about people based solely on their actions or behaviors.
(2) Recognize that someone's eagerness or enthusiasm may be the driving force behind their actions, rather than indicating incompetence or a lack of skill.
(3) Acknowledge and respect the preferences and indulgences of other individuals, such as enjoying a lot of wine, without labeling them as "bad" at it.
(4) Take the time to understand the motives and reasoning behind someone's actions before making any judgements.
(5) To avoid being influenced solely by appearances or superficial observations, it is crucial to keep an open mind and be willing to consider various perspectives.
(6) Make more informed decisions by gaining a more profound understanding of others' perspectives and actions.
(7) Avoid making assumptions about someone's abilities or skills without thoroughly understanding their reasons and motivations.
(8) Foster empathy and understanding by cultivating curiosity and asking questions to gain insight into the actions and preferences of others.

Embodying Philosophical Principles through Actions

46. Never label yourself as a philosopher and avoid discussing your philosophical beliefs with non-experts. Instead, embody the principles you hold dear through your actions. For instance, at a social gathering, do not lecture about how people should eat; simply eat respectfully. Follow the example of Socrates, who was so humble that people sought him out to meet philosophers and try to avoid seeking attention. If a conversation about philosophy arises among non-experts, it is best to stay quiet. There is a risk of impulsively

Chapter 6 — Mental Fortitude and Appropriate Actions

spewing out ideas that you have not fully thought through. When someone tells you that you know nothing, and it does not bother you, take it as a sign that you are on the right track with your endeavors. Just like sheep do not bring their food to the shepherds to prove how much they have eaten, but instead digest it and produce wool and milk, you should refrain from showing off your philosophical beliefs to non-experts. Let them instead witness the tangible outcomes that result from your well-digested principles.

From lesson...

Embody your philosophical principles through your actions, refrain from seeking attention, stay humble, think before speaking, and let your tangible outcomes speak for themselves.

To action!

(1) Do not label yourself as a philosopher.
(2) It is advisable to avoid engaging in discussions about your philosophical beliefs with individuals who are not experts in the field.
(3) Live out your principles through your actions.
(4) Practice respectful eating at social gatherings without lecturing others.
(5) Strive to be humble, much like Socrates, and avoid the pursuit of attention.
(6) It is advisable to remain silent when engaging in conversations about philosophy with non-experts.
(7) Be cautious about impulsively spewing out thoughtless ideas.
(8) Take it as a positive sign when someone tells you that you know nothing.
(9) Avoid displaying your philosophical beliefs to non-experts.
(10) Allow others to witness the tangible outcomes that result from your well-digested principles.

Embracing Simplicity: The Power of Discretion in Self-Care

47. Once you have adapted to a simple lifestyle in terms of taking care of your bodily needs, there is no need to boast about it. Likewise, if you prefer drinking water over other beverages, there is no need to announce it on every occasion. And if you are seeking to improve your physical endurance, do it for yourself rather than for

Chapter 6 — Mental Fortitude and Appropriate Actions

others to see. There is no need to show off by embracing statues or making a spectacle of yourself. Instead, try a discreet exercise: when you are truly thirsty, take a sip of cold water and discreetly spit it out without drawing attention to it.

From lesson...

Adopt a simple lifestyle, refrain from boasting, keep your healthy habits to yourself, and strive for personal improvement without seeking validation from others.

To action!

(1) When it comes to taking care of your body's needs, try to adapt to a simpler lifestyle.
(2) Do not boast about your adapted lifestyle.
(3) Choose to drink water over other beverages.
(4) Try to avoid constantly proclaiming your preference for water in every situation.
(5) Focus on improving your physical endurance for personal satisfaction, rather than for others to see.
(6) Do not try to impress others by hugging statues or drawing attention to yourself unnecessarily.
(7) Take part in discreet exercises.
(8) If you are feeling really thirsty, go ahead and take a refreshing sip of cold water.
(9) Quietly spit out the water without attracting any attention to yourself.

Seeking Progress: Taking Responsibility and Letting Go of External Influences

48. This is what it is like to be a regular person: they never rely solely on themselves for anything and instead seek help or harm from external factors. On the other hand, a philosopher assumes full responsibility for their own well-being or downfall.

Here are some signs that indicate someone is making progress: they refrain from criticizing, praising, blaming, or finding fault with others. They do not boast about themselves or act as if they know everything. When faced with obstacles, they hold themselves accountable instead of pointing fingers elsewhere. If someone

Chapter 6 — Mental Fortitude and Appropriate Actions

compliments them, they simply smile to themselves, and if someone criticizes them, they do not feel the need to defend themselves. They navigate cautiously, much like someone recovering from an illness, ensuring that they do not disrupt any progress they have made. They have relinquished all their desires and solely focus on avoiding actions that contradict human nature and are within their control. They refrain from making firm decisions about anything. Even if they appear foolish or ignorant, they are unconcerned about the opinions of others. Essentially, they consistently exercise caution in their own actions, treating themselves as their own worst enemy.

From lesson...

Take full responsibility for your own well-being, refrain from relying on external factors, and exercise caution in your actions to make progress and attain true fulfillment.

To action!

(1) Assume complete responsibility for your own personal well-being or potential downfall.
(2) Avoid depending on external factors for assistance or harm, and instead direct your attention towards self-reliance.
(3) Avoid criticizing, praising, blaming, or finding fault with others.
(4) It is important to avoid boasting about oneself or acting like one knows it all.
(5) When confronted with obstacles, it is important to hold yourself accountable rather than shifting blame onto others.
(6) There is no need to feel the need to defend yourself when someone criticizes you.
(7) When someone gives you a compliment, all you need to do is simply smile to yourself.
(8) Move around cautiously, as if you were recovering from an illness, to avoid disrupting the progress.
(9) Release yourself from desires and concentrate on refraining from actions that contradict human nature and fall under your authority.
(10) Do not rush into making tough decisions about anything.
(11) Do not care about the opinions of others, even if you may appear foolish or ignorant.

(12) Always be vigilant of your own actions and consider yourself to be your own greatest adversary.

Finding True Understanding: Beyond Interpretation and into Action

49. When someone acts superior because they understand and can explain the writings of Chrysippus, I remind myself, "If Chrysippus had written clearly, this person wouldn't have anything to boast about."

But what is it that I truly desire? To comprehend the natural world and live in harmony with it. Therefore, I seek out someone who can elucidate it for me, and I hear that Chrysippus accomplishes just that. However, when I peruse his writings, I struggle to comprehend them. Consequently, I search for someone who can interpret Chrysippus for me. Until this juncture, there is no reason to take pride. Nevertheless, once I find the interpreter, what truly matters is implementing their teachings into action. That is the only thing worthy of pride. If I solely admire the act of interpretation, then I have become a grammarian rather than a philosopher. The only disparity is that I interpret Chrysippus instead of Homer. Rather than feeling a sense of pride, when someone asks me to explicate Chrysippus, I feel ashamed if I cannot demonstrate actions that align with his words.

From lesson...

Seek understanding and wisdom from those who can interpret and guide you in living harmoniously with the natural world.

To action!

(1) Strive to seek understanding of the natural world and live in accordance with it.
(2) Seek out someone who can skillfully elucidate the teachings of Chrysippus.
(3) Look for an interpreter who can assist in clarifying Chrysippus' writings.
(4) Put the teachings of the interpreter into action in your own life.
(5) Instead of merely admiring the act of interpretation, it is more beneficial to direct our focus towards the practical application of Chrysippus' teachings.

(6) The aim is to demonstrate actions that are consistent with Chrysippus' teachings when questioned about them.
(7) Don't feel embarrassed if you cannot explain Chrysippus; instead, concentrate on showing how his teachings are applied through your actions.

Embracing Unbreakable Principles and Ignoring Opinions of Others

50. Stick to your principles as if they were unbreakable rules, honoring the fact that going against them would be disrespectful. However, do not worry about others' opinions of you, as in the end, you have no control over them.

From lesson...

Hold on to your principles firmly and disregard the opinions of others, as their thoughts are beyond your control.

To action!

(1) Identify your principles: Take the time to reflect on your core values and beliefs that guide your actions.
(2) Prioritize your principles: Determine which principles are most important to you and align them with your goals and aspirations.
(3) Define your unbreakable rules: Clearly establish boundaries and non-negotiables that are rooted in your principles.
(4) Stay committed: Remind yourself regularly of your principles and consciously make an effort to adhere to them in your daily life.
(5) Be self-aware: Reflect on your actions and decisions to ensure that they are in line with your principles and make any necessary adjustments if needed.
(6) Embrace respectful dissent. While it is essential to hold on to your principles, remain open to hearing diverse perspectives and engaging in respectful discussions.
(7) Focus on self-validation: Instead of seeking validation and approval from others, trust in the validity of your principles and values.
(8) Practice resilience: Accept that not everyone will agree with or understand your principles and develop the resilience to stay true to them despite external opinions.

(9) Communicate your principles by sharing them with others when appropriate. Explain to them why these principles are important to you and how they influence your actions.

(10) Lead by example: Demonstrate through your actions and behaviors how your principles positively impact not only your own life, but also the lives of those around you.

> **Claim Your Worth and Achieve Progress: Embrace Self-Improvement and Live with Purpose**

51. How long will you continue to wait before believing in your own worthiness to experience the best things in life, without crossing any boundaries set by reason? You have already acquired the principles of philosophy and have accepted them. So, why do you still await someone else to teach you before embarking on your personal growth journey? You are no longer a child, but an adult. If you continue to be lazy and procrastinate, always making excuses and delaying self-improvement, you will make no progress. Instead, you will simply navigate through life without achieving anything significant. Therefore, make a decision now, before it is too late, to live as a mature individual who constantly strives for progress. Let everything you believe is best for you become a guiding principle that you never compromise. And when you encounter something difficult, enjoyable, popular, or unpopular, remember that this is the moment to prove yourself. It is like the Olympics, and you cannot postpone any longer. The outcome of a single day and a single action will determine whether you make progress or not. Look at how Socrates became the person he was by always relying on reason in the face of challenges. Even if you have not reached Socrates' level yet, you should still live as someone who aspires to be like him.

From lesson...

Believe in your own worthiness, nurture personal growth, strive for progress, and rely on reason to achieve significant success in life.

To action!

(1) Believe in your own worthiness of the best things in life and establish boundaries for yourself that are grounded in reason.

(2) Take responsibility for your own self-improvement and begin working on it without waiting for someone else to guide you.
(3) To avoid laziness and procrastination, it is important to actively pursue self-improvement and refrain from making excuses.
(4) Make a conscious decision to live your life as a mature individual who is always pursuing progress.
(5) Make what you believe is best for you become a guiding principle that you never contradict.
(6) Embrace and challenge yourself in difficult, yet enjoyable situations, regardless of whether they are popular or unpopular, to prove your capabilities.
(7) Approach each day and every action as a chance for advancement and personal development.
(8) Take inspiration from figures like Socrates, who relied on reason in every situation they encountered.
(9) Always aspire to improve and strive to attain greater levels of wisdom and knowledge, just like Socrates.

Living by Philosophical Principles

52. The first and most crucial aspect of philosophy revolves around the application of principles to our lives. For instance, one principle is to never tell lies. The second part involves comprehending the underlying reasons for these principles. So, why is it considered wrong to lie? The third part assists us in discerning between different ideas and establishing proof. We inquire about matters such as "How do we ascertain the truth? What constitutes a logical argument? What defines right and wrong?" The third part is necessary due to the second, and the second is necessary due to the first. However, here is the issue - we tend overly to prioritize the third part and overlook the significance of the first. We invest all our time in debates and arguments, neglecting to actually live according to the principles we claim to hold. This is why we often find ourselves resorting to lying but are quick to conjure up arguments to justify why lying is unacceptable.

Chapter 6 — Mental Fortitude and Appropriate Actions

> *From lesson...*
>
> Apply principles to your life, understand their significance, and live by them instead of getting caught up in endless debates and justifications.

> **To action!**

(1) Apply principles to our lives: Take the time to reflect on the principles we believe in and actively apply them in our daily lives. This might include making a deliberate effort to never tell lies, as mentioned in the text.

(2) Understand the reasons behind principles: Invest time in understanding the underlying reasons and justifications for the principles we claim to believe in. This may involve researching and reflecting on why lying is considered wrong.

(3) To establish a framework for distinguishing between ideas, it is important to develop a systematic approach to evaluating different ideas and arguments. This could involve asking critical questions, such as "How do we know this is true?" and "What constitutes a logical argument?"

(4) Strive for logical consistency by seeking to align our beliefs and actions in a logical and consistent manner. This might require us to question whether our actions are truly in line with the principles we claim to believe in.

(5) Prioritize living by your principles: Dedicate sufficient time and energy to living according to your principles, rather than solely engaging in debates and arguments. Avoid neglecting the practical application of your beliefs in favor of intellectual discussions.

(6) Act with integrity: Abide by our principles and make a conscious effort to be truthful in both our actions and our words. Refrain from seeking excuses or using arguments to justify behaviors that contradict our values, such as lying.

(7) Regular self-reflection: It is important to regularly take the time to reflect on our actions and assess if they align with the principles we claim to adhere to. This practice can assist in identifying areas where improvement is necessary, which in turn promotes personal growth.

Chapter 6 — Mental Fortitude and Appropriate Actions

(8) Encourage self-awareness: Cultivate a strong sense of self-awareness to recognize when we are deviating from our principles or engaging in behaviors that contradict our beliefs. This practice can effectively ensure consistency between our beliefs and actions.

(9) Foster open dialogue by engaging in meaningful conversations and discussions that promote understanding and reflection, rather than solely focusing on arguments and debates. Encourage others to live by their beliefs and principles as well.

(10) Practice empathy and understanding: Strive to comprehend various perspectives and viewpoints, even during debates or discussions. This can contribute to nurturing a more compassionate approach when implementing principles in our lives.

The Power of Spiritual Connection and Resilience

53. In every situation, we should keep the following thoughts in mind:

"Guide me, O higher power, and the forces that shape my destiny, towards the path that was set for me a long time ago. I will remain committed and unwavering, even if my determination falters."

"If someone accepts and embraces the inevitable, we consider them wise and deeply connected to the spiritual realm."

"Well, my dear friend Crito, if the gods deem it favorable, then so be it."

"Anytus and Meletus may have the power to take my life, but they cannot harm the essence of my being."

From lesson...

Stay committed and steadfast, embracing the inevitable and trusting in higher guidance, for external circumstances may change, but the essence of your being remains unaffected.

To action!

(1) Maintain a powerful sense of commitment and steadfastness, even when faced with wavering determination.

(2) Embrace and accept the inevitable, demonstrating wisdom and spiritual connection.

(3) Seek guidance from a higher power and the forces that shape your destiny.

(4) Stay connected to your true essence, regardless of external circumstances or threats.

(5) If the gods favor a particular outcome, accept it willingly.

(6) Stay true to one's path and destiny, which was set a long time ago.

INDEX

abilities, 8, 14, 15, 42, 56, 57, 62, 64, 65, 67, 68, 69
accept, 3, 7, 11, 12, 16, 17, 23, 25, 35, 37, 47, 49, 51, 78, 79
acceptance, 12, 17, 23, 29
accepting, 12, 23, 24, 40, 45, 46, 47, 56, 57
access, 38, 39
accidents happen, 36, 37
accomplishments, 8, 9, 20, 28, 32, 62
accountability, 38, 53
accurate reflection, 28
accusing, 46
achieve, 2, 10, 15, 27, 34, 42, 52, 58, 75
achievements, 7, 8, 9, 20, 49, 51, 62, 63
achieving triumph, 52
acknowledge, 2, 3, 5, 7, 9, 36, 37, 49, 51, 57, 68
act, 9, 13, 19, 28, 40, 61, 65, 71, 73
action, 38, 54, 57, 58, 73, 75, 76
actions, 1, 2, 3, 11, 13, 17, 18, 19, 22, 28, 31, 32, 34, 38, 41, 54, 55, 56, 58, 64, 67, 68, 69, 70, 72, 74, 75, 77, 78
activities, 12, 14, 33, 38, 39, 40, 49, 58, 62, 63, 64, 66, 68
actor, 25
acts of goodness, 38
adapt, 60, 71
adaptability, 17

adjust, 12
adjustments, 26, 74
admiration, 30, 35
advancement, 76
advantageous, 26
adversity, 13, 15
advice, 34, 45, 47, 48, 56, 61, 65
advocate, 14, 63
affection, 5
agitated, 6
alcohol consumption, 64
align, 13, 19, 26, 42, 56, 58, 59, 61, 64, 73, 74, 77
allegiance, 48
allocate, 7, 56
allure, 52, 53
alternatives, 35
analyze, 2, 3, 28
anger, 16, 65
announce, 70
appearance, 61, 62, 63
apply, 11, 23, 24, 36, 77
appreciate, 9, 16, 23, 30, 48, 52, 68
appreciation, 17, 55
approach, 6, 22, 23, 24, 47, 54, 64, 66, 77, 78
appropriate proportion, 59
arguments, 76, 77, 78
arms, 41
art, 30, 39
ashamed, 32, 73
aspects of your life, 13, 26
aspirations, 2, 3, 64, 74

INDEX

aspire, 40, 76
assertiveness training, 39
assess, 19, 42, 56, 59, 77
assigned role, 25
assistance, 32, 33, 72
assumptions, 24, 69
atmosphere, 55
attachments, 12, 16
attention, 9, 19, 28, 35, 55, 57, 58, 63, 64, 67, 68, 69, 70, 71, 72
authentic, 13, 32, 65
authentic self, 13
authenticity, 8, 19, 68
available, 10, 34
aversions, 11, 46, 47
avoid, 4, 6, 7, 21, 22, 24, 27, 29, 31, 35, 36, 37, 46, 48, 49, 50, 51, 54, 56, 59, 66, 69, 70, 71, 72, 76
avoiding excess, 61
awful, 29
bad, 21, 32, 41, 45, 46, 68, 69
balance, 19, 34, 55, 56, 61
balanced approach, 29, 64
based, 36, 48, 58, 61, 65, 68, 69
bathing routine, 68
bathroom, 63, 64
battles, 65
beggar, 25
behavior, 7, 18, 35, 38, 42, 43, 48, 49, 50, 51, 53, 61
behaviors, 22, 69, 75, 77, 78
being, 1, 2, 5, 9, 13, 18, 19, 21, 25, 27, 30, 32, 33, 35, 39, 45, 47, 49, 51, 52, 55, 56, 59, 68, 69, 78
beliefs, 7, 19, 20, 30, 32, 45, 46, 54, 65, 66, 70, 74, 77, 78
believe in, 54, 77
belongings, 1, 24, 36, 59, 60, 67
beneficial, 4, 26, 33, 46, 73
best, 15, 25, 48, 49, 51, 54, 55, 57, 66, 69, 75, 76
bigger picture, 9, 10
bigger portion, 55
blacksmith, 33
blame, 2, 3, 7, 16, 45, 72
blaming, 3, 7, 46, 71, 72

blushing, 49, 51
boasting, 7, 71, 72
bodies, 1, 13, 15
body image, 62, 63
bonds, 26
book clubs, 64
bounce back, 28
boundaries, 40, 53, 58, 66, 74, 75
bowel movements, 64
bragging, 49, 50, 51
break, 5, 15, 36
breakages, 37
breathe, 28
brief, 25
bring, 5, 12, 28, 29, 38, 58, 70
brings positivity, 26
broaden, 20, 64
build resilience, 66
building resilience, 39
Caesar, 41
calls for action, 10
capabilities, 31, 56, 76
captain, 9, 10
caring, 19
carried away, 27, 52, 53
catch, 67
caught up, 9, 10, 48, 50, 77
cautious, 24, 27, 49, 51, 52, 57, 70
challenge, 15, 20, 62, 63, 66, 76
challenges, 6, 8, 11, 12, 14, 15, 23, 28, 40, 41, 42, 62, 75
challenging circumstances, 16, 26
challenging conversations, 63
change in perspective, 45
chaos, 6, 39, 40
character, 13, 25, 62
child, 5, 9, 16, 24, 36, 40, 75
children, 21, 22, 23
choices, 1, 2, 4, 13, 19, 51, 54, 58, 61
choose, 6, 8, 12, 25, 26, 35, 36, 41, 49
circumstances, 3, 7, 17
claim, 7, 8, 76, 77
cleanliness, 49, 50
clear, 26, 36, 40, 41, 48, 50, 53, 66
clear boundaries, 66

INDEX

clear your mind, 26
clueless, 18, 19
cobbler, 33
collaboration, 57
commitment, 13, 30, 42
committed, 40, 74, 78
common ground, 67
communicate, 54, 57, 65, 66
communities, 54
community, 12, 14, 38, 63
community involvement, 63
comparing, 67, 68
compassion, 36, 37, 65
compassionate dialogue, 68
compete, 40, 42, 46
competition, 27
compliments, 72
comprehend, 73, 78
compromise, 19, 34, 36, 56, 75
concentrate, 5, 22, 28, 72, 74
concept, 19, 29, 31, 59, 68
concise, 48, 50
conclusion, 9, 15
condition, 13, 14
confidence, 28, 47, 48, 54, 63
confident, 19, 39
conflicts, 66, 67
confront, 37
connect, 58, 68
connected, 26, 46, 58, 78
consent, 62
consequences, 34, 47, 48, 52, 59
consider, 5, 6, 12, 31, 34, 36, 40, 41, 47, 48, 52, 55, 57, 58, 59, 60, 68, 69, 73, 78
considerate, 66
consideration, 26, 40, 66
consistent character, 48, 50
constructive conversations, 67
constructive criticism, 8, 54
consume, 40
contemplate, 13, 17, 26, 40
contentment, 11, 12, 16, 29, 31, 32, 52, 53
contradict human nature, 72
contribution, 56

control, 1, 2, 3, 4, 5, 7, 12, 18, 21, 22, 25, 27, 28, 32, 33, 35, 36, 39, 45, 46, 47, 72, 74
control over the outcome, 27
controllable, 4
convenience, 60
conversation, 6, 48, 50, 57, 62, 65, 69
conversations, 20, 29, 37, 49, 50, 51, 70, 78
coping mechanisms, 28, 62
core values, 6, 19, 61, 74
counseling services, 62
counselors, 29
country, 33, 34, 47, 48
courses, 56
create a plan, 53
critical thinking, 38, 62, 64
criticism, 30, 39
criticisms, 65
criticize, 54
criticizing, 48, 71, 72
crucial, 1, 4, 5, 9, 10, 12, 13, 14, 15, 19, 28, 37, 42, 50, 55, 56, 57, 61, 67, 69, 76
crude jokes, 50
cultivate, 14, 15, 16, 17, 26, 29, 62, 68
cultivate gratitude, 16, 29
curiosity, 69
daily practice, 29
danger, 47
dangers, 48
death, 4, 6, 7, 29, 30
debates, 76, 77, 78
deceiving themselves, 64
decency, 11
decision, 19, 25, 40, 47, 54, 75, 76
decision regarding your character, 25
decision-making, 19
decisions, 1, 19, 22, 23, 54, 57, 58, 72, 74
decluttering, 59
deep breathing, 39
defend, 49, 50, 51, 72
defend oneself against rumors, 50

INDEX

defend themselves, 72
define, 13, 60
defined, 67
delayed gratification, 53
delegation, 57
demands, 9, 34
demonstrate actions, 73, 74
desires, 1, 2, 3, 4, 11, 12, 21, 22, 29, 42, 46, 47, 72
destiny, 30, 37, 78, 79
detachment, 16, 18
determination, 8, 13, 78
devastated, 5
develop, 8, 14, 15, 28, 29, 30, 39, 62, 63, 65, 74, 77
development, 8, 19, 20, 62, 63, 64, 68
devotion, 45, 46
difference, 33, 38
difficult situations, 8
digest, 70
dilemma, 55
dining partner, 55
dinner party, 22, 23, 35
dinner table, 55
Diogenes, 23, 24
disabled person, 25
disappointed, 34, 52
disappointment, 11, 21, 22, 29, 35, 52
disapproval, 49, 51
disapprove, 54
disciplined, 40
discourage, 30
discreet exercise, 71
discussions, 20, 70, 74, 77, 78
disdain, 41
disease, 4
disrespect, 40
disruptions, 6, 7
disrupts, 6
dissatisfaction, 29, 36
dissent, 74
distorted understanding, 64
distraction, 52
distractions, 10, 53
distress, 24

disturb, 18, 56
diversity, 68
divination, 47, 48
diving in, 6, 40
doctor, 40, 42
downsizing, 59
drawbacks, 36
drawing attention, 71
drinking cup, 36
drinking habits, 41
drinking water, 70
duty, 10, 42, 47, 48, 64
duty calls, 10
dwell, 10, 16, 49
dwelling, 12, 16, 36, 51, 67
easily characterized, 68
eaten, 70
eating habits, 42
education, 37, 62
education systems, 62
effort, 2, 3, 15, 29, 35, 36, 49, 56, 65, 74, 77
efforts, 2, 9, 22, 55, 57
elucidate, 73
embarrass, 56
embarrassed, 39, 74
embody, 21, 69
embrace, 11, 12, 13, 46
embracing, 5, 23, 24, 68, 71, 78
embracing statues, 71
emotional challenges, 40
emotional maturity, 50
emotional responses, 21
emotional strength, 39
emotional well-being, 40
emotions, 21, 28, 29, 30, 39
empathy, 14, 25, 28, 37, 38, 65, 67, 68, 69, 78
employees, 17, 18
emulate, 41
encourage, 13, 20, 38, 39
endeavors, 70
endless, 77
endurance, 14, 15
enemies, 2, 3, 46
energy, 1, 4, 12, 16, 29, 77

INDEX

engage, 5, 14, 33, 49, 50, 51, 63, 64, 65
engage in meaningful conversations, 50
engaged, 10
engrossed, 10
enhance, 8, 14, 21, 26, 40, 53, 54, 56, 57, 59, 64, 68
enjoy, 10
enthusiastic, 40
envy, 27
equal emphasis, 3
essence, 5, 78
establishing boundaries, 39
Eteocles, 46
Euphrates, 41
evaluate, 2, 21, 36, 53, 56, 60
evaluating, 77
events, 12, 21, 24, 32, 64
every situation, 26, 66, 71, 76, 78
evil, 37, 38, 45, 47
examination, 41
examine, 7, 43
examples, 24, 34
excel, 56
excellence, 25
excessive desires, 29
excessive indulgence, 59
excessive laughter, 50
executive, 25
exercise caution, 52, 72
existence, 37, 45
expand, 56
expectations, 12, 18, 56, 58, 62
experience, 8, 18, 42, 43, 52, 56, 57, 59, 61, 75
experiences, 14, 20, 24, 30, 58, 60, 65
expertise, 20, 56
experts, 8, 69, 70
explain, 73, 74
explicate, 73
exploration, 11
exploring, 9
external appearances, 27
external circumstances, 1, 3, 18, 49, 78, 79

external factors, 1, 2, 6, 33, 41, 45, 46, 71, 72
external influences, 3, 14, 16, 28, 29, 39
external nature, 3
external recognition, 20, 34
external validation, 8, 33, 39
externally, 32, 41, 42
extravagance, 59
extravagant buildings, 33
failing to achieve, 4
failure, 20
failures, 54
fairness, 38, 45
faith, 17, 54, 58
faithfulness, 33, 34
fallen short, 57
familiarity, 39
family, 9, 13, 42, 46, 65, 67
fancy events, 32, 33
farm, 16
farmers, 46
fate of humanity, 36
father, 42, 43
faults, 7, 21, 49, 51
favorable, 25, 26, 78
favorite mug, 5
feedback, 8, 19, 54, 56
fellow citizens, 43
fidelity, 34
finances, 23
financial success, 34
finding fault, 71, 72
finding inner peace, 12, 18
finite, 30
fixating, 3, 16, 20, 28, 66
flawed, 65
flaws, 22
focused, 6, 9, 29, 53
fondness, 5
food, 48, 49, 50, 55, 70
force, 2, 22, 23, 69
forces, 78
forgiveness, 40, 65
foster, 68
framework, 77
free person, 27

INDEX

freedom, 1, 3, 17, 21, 27, 41, 42
fresh water, 9
frustrated, 2, 12
frustration, 6
fulfill, 10, 33, 45, 56
fulfillment, 29, 31, 32, 34, 52, 60, 72
fully present, 52
functionality, 59
future, 38, 57, 58
future generations, 38
gain insight, 67, 69
genuine assistance, 34
gifts, 16, 17
given back, 16, 17
Giver, 16
goal, 3, 6, 9, 30, 40, 45
goals, 2, 3, 6, 10, 15, 19, 20, 22, 41, 42, 53, 62, 64, 74
gods, 45, 46, 47, 48, 78, 79
gods favor, 79
going beyond, 68
good, 7, 21, 23, 33, 41, 42, 45, 46, 47
gossip, 50
gossiping, 48
grace, 17, 23
grammarian, 73
grand plan, 17
gratitude, 12, 24
greater satisfaction, 53
greatest adversary, 73
grounded, 19, 29, 57, 75
grounding exercises, 39
group discussions, 64
grudges, 40, 65
guidance, 29, 34, 47, 48, 58, 61, 67, 78
guide, 13, 49, 62, 73, 74, 76
gut feelings, 57
handle, 5, 7, 14, 15, 40, 46, 49, 50, 51, 65, 66
handle important situations with dignity, 50
happiness, 2, 3, 18, 27, 31, 60
hard work, 8, 41

harm, 2, 3, 28, 38, 42, 43, 46, 71, 72, 78
harmful, 46, 62, 63
harmonious atmosphere, 55, 56
harms, 27, 28, 43
harness, 48
hazard, 10
healing process, 16
health, 14
healthier perspective, 30
healthy relationships, 62
heavy drinking, 63, 64
Heraclitus, 23, 24
hesitation, 10
high social status, 27
higher power, 17, 45, 78
higher quality, 67
highly regarded, 27
hinder, 3, 13, 16
historical figures, 23
hold themselves accountable, 71
Homer, 73
honestly, 41, 57
honor, 32, 33
hopeless, 29
horse, 7
host, 35, 55
human condition, 30
human experience, 29
humble, 19, 69, 70
humility, 8, 19, 57, 61
hunger, 17, 18, 55, 63
ideas, 76, 77
Identify, 19, 38, 59, 74
identity, 39, 67
ignorant, 7, 72
ignored, 37, 49, 58
illness, 13, 14, 72
imagine, 6
impact, 2, 15, 19, 24, 28, 29, 39, 55, 59, 60, 63, 75
impede, 3, 13, 48
imperfections, 22
impermanence, 17, 29
importance, 11, 18, 27, 31, 45, 61, 62, 68

86

INDEX

important, 1, 2, 3, 6, 9, 10, 14, 15, 18, 19, 21, 23, 24, 27, 28, 30, 32, 34, 36, 37, 40, 41, 42, 43, 45, 49, 50, 51, 53, 55, 56, 57, 59, 64, 65, 66, 68, 69, 72, 74, 75, 76, 77
impressing others, 18, 19, 36
improve, 15, 70, 76
improving, 68, 71
impulsive behavior, 41, 42
impulsive desires, 61
impulsive reactions, 28
impulsively, 69, 70
inclusive, 14, 68
inclusivity, 38
inconveniences, 18, 37
indifferent, 47
individual contributions, 34
individuality, 22, 62
individuals, 9, 14, 30, 36, 38, 40, 43, 46, 50, 57, 58, 60, 68, 69, 70
indulgence, 52
indulging, 68
influence, 1, 4, 23, 24, 26, 29, 50, 55, 75
influenced, 1, 3, 27, 69
informed decisions, 69
initial impressions, 21
injuries, 40, 42
injustice, 38
inner freedom, 61
inner guidance, 57, 58
inner peace, 1, 17, 18, 39
innermost thoughts, 39
insecurities, 28, 62
insights, 20, 29, 34, 54, 56, 57, 58
inspiration, 13, 30, 34, 60, 76
inspire, 13, 14, 20, 32, 54, 58, 62
instincts, 57
insult, 39, 40, 65
insults, 27, 28, 39, 40, 65, 66
integrity, 8, 24, 33, 34, 77
intellect, 63
intellectual attitude, 30
intellectual stimulation, 64
intelligence, 45, 61, 62
intentional decisions, 53

intentional living, 60
internally, 32, 41, 42
interpret, 26, 73
interpretation, 24, 28, 73
interpreter, 73
intertwine, 41
intuition, 57
irrelevant, 47
irritated, 28
issues, 67
jealousy, 27, 35
job, 23
journaling, 58, 64
journey, 14, 17, 75
joy, 5, 12, 29, 32, 52, 60
judge, 27, 68
judgment, 7, 24, 48, 50, 58
judgmental, 49, 51
judgments, 7, 39
juggling, 19
jump to conclusions, 69
justice, 38, 45
justifications, 77
kindness, 11, 23, 38
know nothing, 70
knowledge, 7, 18, 19, 38, 56, 64, 68, 76
label, 68, 69, 70
labeling, 46, 69
lack of skill, 69
laugh, 30, 48
laugh excessively, 48
lawful activities, 51
laziness, 76
lazy, 75
leadership roles, 63
lecture, 69
lectures, 64
lecturing, 70
length of the play, 25
let go, 2, 4, 9, 10, 16, 29, 47, 65
letting go, 3, 12, 59
level-headed mindset, 11
lies, 76, 77
life, 8, 9, 10, 11, 12, 13, 14, 15, 16, 17, 18, 22, 23, 24, 26, 29, 30,

INDEX

32, 35, 36, 37, 42, 53, 59, 60, 63, 64, 73, 74, 75, 76, 77, 78
like-minded individuals, 20, 54
limitations, 3, 8, 13, 56, 57
limited, 65
limits, 53
linguistic abilities, 68
literature, 30
little things, 9, 10
live, 11, 13, 14, 17, 21, 29, 32, 73, 75, 76, 77, 78
live in harmony, 73
lives, 1, 22, 45, 61, 75, 76, 77, 78
loftier aspirations, 3
logical argument, 76, 77
logical consistency, 77
logical solution, 47, 48
long-term fulfillment, 53
loss, 16, 17, 37, 46
losses, 16, 17, 18
lost, 16
loved one, 5, 16, 22, 25, 26, 28, 37, 46, 53
loved ones, 5, 16, 22, 25, 26, 28, 46, 53
loving partner, 9
lower social status, 41
loyalty, 33, 47, 48
luxurious baths, 33
maintain, 6, 11, 15, 26, 29, 33, 34, 41, 42, 43, 45, 49, 50, 51, 55, 56, 59, 60, 64, 65, 67
making decisions, 5, 48
making firm decisions, 72
manner of speech, 67
marriage, 49, 51
material goods, 34
material possessions, 18, 25, 26, 49, 50, 67, 68
material success, 2, 3, 34
mature individual, 75, 76
meal, 55, 56
meaning, 14, 31
meaningful aspects, 67
meaningful subjects, 48
meanings, 55
media, 62, 63

media literacy, 63
mediation, 67
meditation, 12, 29, 39, 58, 64, 66
meditation techniques, 29
men, 61, 62
mental and intellectual growth, 64
mental exercise, 63
mental wellbeing, 39
mental well-being, 14
mental well-being, 64
mental well-being, 66
mentor, 12, 42, 58
mentors, 8, 20, 34, 56, 65
mentorship programs, 62
merchants, 46
mere appearances, 69
messy, 49
milk, 70
mind, 2, 9, 10, 12, 14, 17, 25, 29, 39, 63, 65, 78
mindful, 19, 46, 50, 53, 55, 56, 57, 59, 63, 68
mindful communication, 68
mindful consumption, 59
mindful eating, 63
mindfulness, 12, 29, 39, 52, 57, 58, 64, 66
mindfulness practices, 64
mindset, 1, 3, 8, 11, 12, 16, 17, 18, 23, 26, 31, 43, 45, 46, 49, 53, 67
minimalism, 60
misfortune, 4
mistakes, 7, 20, 40, 65
mistreat, 43, 65
mistreatment, 38, 65, 66, 67
mistreats, 42, 64, 65, 66
mobility, 13
mock, 30
moderation, 61, 64
modern lives, 11
moment, 2, 5, 6, 7, 9, 13, 14, 17, 25, 26, 28, 36, 39, 40, 41, 42, 52, 53, 58, 67, 75
moment to pause, 26, 28, 52
moment to reflect, 5, 7, 14, 26, 36, 39, 52, 67
money, 1, 17, 23, 33, 67, 68

INDEX

moral compass, 13, 34, 45
moral principles, 43
moral values, 13, 42
morals, 13, 14, 54
mortality, 22, 30
motivations, 69
motives, 19, 68, 69
multifaceted, 68
natural flow, 17, 61
natural world, 73
nature, 5, 17, 25, 36, 42, 58
nature of your character, 25
navigate, 11, 12, 17, 19, 29, 34, 65, 72, 75
necessary actions, 26
negative, 2, 3, 6, 22, 28, 29, 32, 34, 40, 50, 52, 64, 65, 66, 67
negative emotions, 40
negative experiences, 28, 66
negative external influences, 2, 3
negative influences, 50
negative outcomes, 52
negative things, 64
negative words, 65
negatively impact, 55, 65
negativity, 39
neglect, 17, 19, 46, 56
neglecting, 45, 56, 76, 77
negligence, 18
neighbors, 43
network, 20, 65
new experiences, 12, 23, 24
new skills, 8, 64
non-attachment, 17
non-experts, 69, 70
notable events, 10
notion, 17, 68
nourishing, 64
nurture, 58, 68, 75
oaths, 50
obeying, 45, 46
objective, 6, 9, 56
objects, 4
obligations, 10, 43, 45
obstacles, 6, 7, 13, 15, 71, 72
offensive, 49, 51
oil spills, 17

older, 9, 10
older person, 9
Olympic victory, 40, 41
Olympics, 75
omens, 47
on the right track, 70
open communication, 67
open dialogue, 62, 78
open mind, 24, 47, 68, 69
opening chapter, 1
openly, 57, 62
open-minded, 20
opinions, 6, 7, 19, 20, 33, 39, 58, 72, 74
opponents, 40
opportunities, 8, 12, 19, 23, 24, 53, 56, 58, 60, 62, 63, 68
opportunity, 7, 12, 20, 55, 65
ordinary individual, 25
organizations, 38
others, 2, 3, 7, 8, 11, 14, 15, 18, 19, 20, 22, 23, 27, 28, 29, 30, 31, 32, 33, 34, 35, 36, 37, 38, 39, 41, 43, 45, 48, 49, 50, 51, 54, 57, 58, 60, 65, 67, 68, 69, 70, 71, 72, 74, 75, 78
outcome, 26, 47, 48, 49, 51, 75
overeating, 63
overpower, 30, 52, 53
own actions, 18, 42, 43, 72, 73
ownership, 2, 28
pain, 46
particular outcome, 79
parties, 48, 50, 57
passed away, 16, 36
past experiences, 52, 54, 58
path, 3, 8, 34, 35, 36, 41, 42, 78, 79
patience, 14, 15, 23
pause, 52, 58
peace, 11, 17, 18, 41, 42
peace of mind, 17, 18
peaceful mind, 12, 17, 18
peaceful mindset, 12
pentathlon contender, 41
perceive, 19, 21, 25, 26, 31, 32, 45
perform, 15, 25, 40, 57
perform effectively, 57

89

INDEX

performance, 25, 51, 56
permission, 42, 43
personal beliefs, 25, 26
personal choices, 49, 51
personal development, 19, 40, 51, 64, 68, 76
personal freedom, 27
personal growth, 3, 7, 8, 12, 19, 32, 33, 34, 40, 49, 50, 60, 62, 64, 65, 68, 75, 77
personal hardships, 37
personal impact, 3
personal improvement, 64, 71
personal progress, 20
personal qualities, 34
personal values, 13, 34
perspective, 5, 12, 16, 28, 46, 64, 65, 66, 67
perspectives, 19, 20, 54, 56, 68, 69, 74
philosopher, 30, 32, 40, 42, 47, 69, 70, 71, 73
philosophical beliefs, 69, 70
philosophical principles, 70
philosophy, 23, 30, 41, 48, 50, 69, 70, 75, 76
physical abilities, 13
physical endurance, 70, 71
physical health, 26, 64
physical needs, 55
physical well-being, 1, 25, 26
physique, 41
piety, 46
placing importance, 27
plans, 6, 12
playwright, 25
Playwright, 25
please others, 19, 33
pleasure, 46, 52, 53
Polyneices, 46
pool, 6
portion sizes, 63
position, 1, 41, 51
positive ambiance, 56
positive aspects, 26, 66
positive attitude, 15
positive impact, 11, 14

positive influences, 13, 39, 58
positive mindset, 13, 15, 18
positive outlook, 16
positive relationship, 67
positive self-image, 28
positive self-talk, 28
positivity, 38
possess, 21, 22, 26, 32, 42, 68
possessions, 16, 17, 58, 59, 60, 67
potential, 5, 6, 19, 24, 36, 38, 40, 42, 48, 51, 52, 54, 56, 57, 72
potential consequences, 54
potential downfall, 72
potential risks, 48
poverty, 4
power, 1, 2, 5, 21, 22, 23, 24, 27, 28, 46, 47, 51, 78
powerful, 32, 33, 49, 51, 78
practical application, 73, 77
praise, 27, 35
praised, 27
praising, 48, 71, 72
precautions, 54
preference, 68, 71
preferences, 1, 69
preferential treatment, 34, 35
prepare, 5, 6, 49, 56
prepared, 2, 9, 10, 30, 40, 42, 51
preparing, 6, 55
presence of evil, 37
present moment, 12, 17, 29, 58
pressure, 4, 5
prestigious positions, 32, 33
prevent unhappiness, 4
price, 17, 35
pride, 7, 73
primary responsibility, 25
principles, 6, 13, 14, 19, 30, 34, 60, 69, 70, 74, 75, 76, 77, 78
prioritize, 9, 10, 18, 19, 20, 33, 34, 42, 43, 45, 53, 56, 58, 59, 62, 66, 76
prioritizing, 50, 55, 60
prioritizing essential possessions, 50
problems, 7, 28, 35
procrastinate, 10, 75
produce, 70

INDEX

professional growth, 56
professionals, 29
profound understanding, 43, 69
programs, 62
progress, 3, 17, 18, 20, 48, 53, 71, 72, 75, 76
promote, 37, 58, 63, 66, 78
proof, 76
proportion, 58, 59
prosperity, 34
protect, 26, 39, 58
prove, 19, 70, 75, 76
public readings, 49, 51
public shows, 49, 51
punish, 17
purchases, 59
purity, 49, 50, 51
purity in relationships, 50, 51
purpose, 5, 11, 14, 31, 33, 59
purposefully, 61
pursuing philosophy, 30
pursuit of attention, 70
pursuit of inner peace, 18
puzzles, 63
Pythian Apollo, 47, 48
qualities, 33, 34, 37, 42, 68
raise awareness, 37
ranking, 68
raven ominously caws, 25
reach, 9, 10
reactions, 18, 43
reading, 63, 64
ready, 9, 10
reality of evil, 37
reason, 47, 48, 73, 75, 76
reasoning, 17, 47, 68, 69
reasons, 24, 67, 69, 76, 77
recognition, 8, 34, 35, 36
redefine, 21, 22
redirect, 4, 19
reevaluating, 57
refine, 53, 54, 58
refined, 67
reflect, 19, 27, 30, 39, 52, 53, 54, 58, 60, 74, 77
refocus, 67

refrain, 3, 7, 21, 24, 33, 49, 51, 70, 71, 72, 76
refraining from bragging or making crude jokes, 50
refreshing sip, 71
refusals, 4
regret, 31, 52
regretful, 52
regular individual, 25
rejection, 24
relationship, 30, 42, 43, 45, 55, 60, 66, 67
relationships, 17, 25, 26, 43, 49, 58, 60, 68
rely on reason, 75
remain composed, 39
remain unaffected, 13
remarks, 48, 50
repeated, 30
repurpose, 60
reputation, 1, 41
requests, 34
resentment, 16, 36, 46, 65
resilience, 8, 13, 15, 17, 28, 39, 40, 53, 74
resilient, 20
resisting temptation, 52, 53
resolution, 66, 67
respect, 23, 33, 38, 42, 45, 46, 49, 50, 51, 55, 61, 69
respectful, 65, 70, 74
respectful eating, 70
respond, 2, 3, 9, 10, 42
responses, 43
responsibilities, 9, 10, 11, 17, 18, 33, 42, 43, 45, 56, 57
responsibility, 7, 22, 25, 32, 71, 72, 76
responsive, 10
restrict, 2
result, 4, 26, 61, 70
rewards, 35, 36, 41
riches, 3
ridicule, 30
right, 16, 22, 23, 30, 31, 46, 52, 53, 54, 59, 61, 64, 76
right and wrong, 76

91

INDEX

risk, 47, 69
risks, 40, 54
role, 8, 11, 25, 32, 33, 34, 42, 56, 57, 62, 63
role given, 25
role models, 34, 62
sacrifice, 33
sacrifices, 18, 35, 36, 41, 42
sadness, 7
safe environment, 38
safe spaces, 62
sailors, 46
satiety signals, 64
satisfaction, 8, 32, 52, 53, 71
satisfactory results, 56
satisfied, 55
scary, 6, 7
schools, 62
scoundrel, 16
scrutinize, 21
seek guidance, 12
seek help, 71
seek support, 13, 29
seeking answers, 47
self, 8, 12, 13, 14, 15, 19, 24, 28, 32, 33, 34, 37, 39, 40, 42, 53, 57, 58, 61, 62, 63, 64, 65, 66, 68, 72, 74, 75, 76, 77, 78
self-aware, 19, 28, 32, 39, 57, 64, 74, 78
self-awareness, 19, 28, 32, 39, 57, 64, 78
self-care, 12, 14, 58, 66
self-compassion, 40
self-confidence, 65
self-control, 14, 15, 53
self-discipline, 53
self-esteem, 28, 39, 61, 62, 65
self-expression, 62
self-help books, 39, 64
self-improvement, 8, 12, 19, 24, 32, 34, 40, 42, 65, 75, 76
self-reflection, 13, 40, 53, 64, 65, 68, 77
self-reliance, 72
self-respect, 33, 34, 62
self-respecting friend, 33

self-validation, 32, 74
self-worth, 28, 32, 39, 61, 62
seminars, 64
senator, 27
sense, 8, 11, 17, 24, 28, 32, 39, 48, 55, 65, 67, 73, 78
sense of commitment, 78
sense of deservingness, 24
sense of responsibility, 17
sentimental value, 5
servant, 41
serve, 5, 7, 26, 33, 59
set a long time ago, 79
setbacks, 12, 13, 14, 18, 40, 42
sex education, 62
sexuality, 61
shape, 14, 22, 78
share, 54
sharing, 14, 37, 55, 75
sheep, 9, 70
shepherds, 70
shifting roles, 41
ship, 9
shoes, 33, 59, 65
short-lived pleasure, 52, 53
shouting, 49, 51
show off, 71
showing, 45, 50, 55, 70, 74
showing disapproval of vulgar language, 50
showing off, 70
significance, 1, 13, 33, 38, 39, 62, 76, 77
significant, 2, 3, 8, 10, 36, 37, 38, 56, 61, 75
silence, 49
silent, 48, 50, 51, 58, 70
silly, 18, 19, 21
simple lifestyle, 70, 71
simply eat, 69
sip of cold water, 71
sitting, 55
situation, 2, 6, 10, 12, 14, 18, 24, 25, 28, 36, 47, 48, 49, 50, 55, 66, 67
situations, 11, 26, 27, 29, 34, 36, 39, 48, 57, 58, 65, 76

92

INDEX

size, 58, 59
skill, 25, 56
skills, 19, 56, 62, 68, 69
slave-boy, 21, 22, 36
sleepless nights, 41, 42
small challenges, 18
smallest things, 5
social connection, 42, 43, 55
social connections, 42, 43
social context, 55, 56
social gathering, 69, 70
social gatherings, 70
social standing, 3
social status, 1, 27
societal norms, 62
Socrates, 6, 49, 69, 70, 75, 76
solely, 3, 18, 19, 31, 34, 51, 61, 62, 63, 66, 68, 69, 71, 72, 73, 77, 78
solitude, 41, 58
solution, 47, 67
someone, 7, 14, 15, 21, 22, 24, 25, 27, 28, 30, 31, 32, 33, 34, 35, 36, 37, 39, 41, 42, 46, 49, 51, 53, 55, 64, 65, 66, 68, 70, 71, 72, 73, 75, 76, 78
someone insults, 14, 15, 28, 64
someone tells you, 49, 70
speak, 41, 48, 50, 51, 67, 70
speak wisely, 50
speaking ill, 49
spectacle, 71
spewing out ideas, 70
spiritual connection, 78
spiritual perspectives, 29
spiritual realm, 78
spit it out, 71
spot, 6
spouse, 5, 16, 22, 23, 36
state, 2, 27, 34
statements, 55, 67
Stay connected, 10, 79
stay quiet, 69
steadfast, 48, 78
steadfastness, 78
step back, 28
steps, 15, 26, 37, 40, 41
stern expression, 49, 51

Stoic philosophy, 1
Stoic wisdom, 11
strangers, 23, 48, 50
strength, 15, 41, 53, 61, 63
strength training exercises, 63
strengths, 28, 32, 56, 62, 68
strict diet, 40, 41
strikes, 13
strive, 13, 19, 32, 36, 41, 58, 63, 65, 71, 75, 76
struggles, 53
struggling, 14, 56, 57
submissive, 42, 43
subservient, 1
succeed, 15
success, 11, 15, 34, 35, 42, 56, 60, 68, 75
successes, 8, 15, 54
succumbing, 52
suffering, 16
suggestions, 56
superficial observations, 69
superficial qualities, 67
superior, 67, 68, 73
superiors, 43
support, 8, 12, 13, 20, 24, 28, 29, 38, 39, 53, 54, 57, 58, 62, 65
support groups, 39, 62
supportive, 12, 14, 20, 39, 62, 65
supportive individuals, 20, 39
surface-level markers, 68
surrender, 12, 17
survival, 49, 50
survivors, 38
sustainable options, 59
swayed, 14, 16, 69
sweets, 40
swim, 6
sympathy, 24
take care, 16, 17, 42
taking care, 14, 16, 55, 70, 71
taking oaths, 48, 50
talent, 63
talents, 8, 41, 42, 62
tangible outcomes, 70
task, 5, 6, 15, 19, 31, 40, 41, 56
tasks, 10, 14, 15, 31, 35, 57

INDEX

tax-gatherer, 41
teachings, 11, 24, 73, 74
tears, 24
techniques, 39
temporary lodging, 16, 17
temptation, 2, 8, 52, 53
tension, 56
therapist, 12, 58
therapists, 29
therapy, 39, 40
thighs, 41
things we cannot control, 1, 27
think before speaking, 70
thirsty, 71
thoroughly, 69
thought through, 70
thoughtful, 41, 53
thoughtful consideration, 41
thoughtless ideas, 70
thoughts, 1, 19, 21, 28, 29, 30, 32, 39, 58, 74, 78
threats, 79
tied up, 9
time, 13, 15, 20, 28, 30, 31, 36, 39, 40, 42, 48, 49, 52, 54, 55, 56, 58, 63, 64, 69, 74, 76, 77, 78
time frames, 52
timeless principles, 11
tough times, 11, 12
toxic individuals, 40
tragedies, 5, 37
tragedy, 5, 36
train consistently, 40
trainer, 40, 42
traits, 68
trajectory, 6
tranquility, 12, 17, 18, 41, 42
travelers, 16, 17
troubled, 17, 18
true essence, 5, 13, 79
true freedom, 2, 3, 22
true happiness, 27
true impact, 3
true nature, 5, 22
truly, 2, 3, 7, 8, 9, 10, 17, 21, 24, 27, 33, 47, 49, 59, 60, 68, 71, 73, 77

trust, 12, 31, 32, 39, 57, 58, 74
trusted individuals, 54, 56
truth, 76
truthful, 77
turn to divination, 47
turned away, 49, 51
uncertainty, 11, 12
undermine, 65
understand, 1, 3, 19, 27, 28, 34, 36, 37, 43, 47, 48, 65, 68, 69, 73, 74, 77
understanding, 1, 3, 5, 14, 20, 29, 32, 36, 37, 38, 43, 45, 46, 64, 65, 66, 68, 69, 73, 77, 78
undertaking, 6
unfair criticism, 54
unfavorable circumstances, 36
unhappiness, 4, 18
unique, 62, 68
unnatural, 4
unnecessary stress, 18
unpleasant, 49, 51
unpredictability, 11, 12
unrealistic expectations, 22
unrest, 2
unstoppable, 27
unsuccessful attempts, 57
unwavering, 30, 78
upset, 5, 39, 40, 49
validation, 20, 31, 32, 60, 61, 71, 74
validity, 65, 74
value, 30, 33, 35, 50, 51, 61, 68
values, 6, 7, 13, 14, 19, 20, 26, 31, 32, 34, 36, 38, 45, 53, 54, 58, 64, 65, 74, 77
various perspectives, 69, 78
version, 68
vice, 21, 22
victims, 38
victory, 52, 53
vigilant, 73
virtuous life, 11
voyage, 9, 10
vulgar language, 49, 51
vulnerable, 1, 3
water, 71

INDEX

wealth, 2, 34, 68
weapons, 33
weather, 40, 41
well-balanced workout routine, 63
well-being, 18, 26, 57, 58, 60, 64, 66, 71, 72
well-digested principles, 70
wine gets stolen, 17
wisdom, 7, 32, 73, 76, 78
wise, 23, 31, 47, 48, 78
wise counselors, 47, 48
witness, 70
wool, 70
words, 14, 15, 24, 39, 73, 77
work on self-improvement, 41
workload, 56
workouts, 63
workshops, 56, 62, 64
worth, 18, 23, 49, 52, 60, 61, 63, 65, 67, 68
worthiness, 75
wrestler, 41
wrongdoing, 38, 66
yoga, 12

Printed in Great Britain
by Amazon